CHRISTIAN, SARACEN AND GENRE IN MEDIEVAL FRENCH LITERATURE

MEDIEVAL HISTORY AND CULTURE
VOLUME 3

STUDIES IN
MEDIEVAL HISTORY AND CULTURE

edited by
Francis G. Gentry
Professor of German
Pennsylvania State University

A ROUTLEDGE SERIES

OTHER BOOKS IN THIS SERIES

1. "AND THEN THE END WILL COME"
Early Latin Christian Interpretations of the Opening of the Seven Seals
Douglas W. Lumsden

2. TOPOGRAPHIES OF GENDER IN MIDDLE HIGH GERMAN ARTHURIAN ROMANCE
Alexandra Sterling-Hellenbrand

CHRISTIAN, SARACEN AND GENRE IN MEDIEVAL FRENCH LITERATURE

Lynn Tarte Ramey

ROUTLEDGE
NEW YORK & LONDON

Published in 2001 by
Routledge
29 West 35th Street
New York, NY 10001

Routledge is an imprint of the Taylor & Francis Group.

Copyright © 2001 by Lynn Tarte Ramey

All rights reserved. No part of this book may be reprinted or reproduced or utilized in any form or by any electronic, mechanical, or other means, now known or hereafter invented, including photocopying and recording, or in any information storage or retrieval system, without written permission from the publishers.

10 9 8 7 6 5 4 3 2 1

Library of Congress Cataloging-in-Publication Data

Ramey, Lynn Tarte, 1964-
    Christian, Saracen and genre in medieval French literature / Lynn Tarte Ramey.
      p. cm. – (Studies in medieval history and literature)
   Includes bibliographical references and index.
   ISBN 0-415-93013-8 (alk. paper)
    1. French literature–To 1500–History and criticism. 2. Christians in literature. 3. Saracens in literature. I. Title. II. Series.

PQ155.R4 R35 2001
840.9'38971–dc21   00-068391

Printed on acid-free, 250 year-life paper
Manufactured in the United States of America

Series Editor Foreword

Far from providing just a musty whiff of yesteryear, research in Medieval Studies enters the new century as fresh and vigorous as never before. Scholars representing all disciplines and generations are consistently producing works of research of the highest caliber, utilizing new approaches and methodologies. Volumes in the Medieval History and Culture series will include studies on individual works and authors of Latin and vernacular literatures, historical personalities and events, theological and philosophical issues, and new critical approaches to medieval literature and culture.

Momentous changes have occurred in Medieval Studies in the past thirty years in teaching as well as in scholarship. Thus the goal of the Medieval History and Culture series is to enhance research in the field by providing an outlet for monographs by scholars in the early stages of their careers on all topics related to the broad scope of Medieval Studies, while at the same time pointing to and highlighting new directions that will shape and define scholarly discourse in the future.

Francis G. Gentry

For Dwayne and Caitlin

CONTENTS

Acknowledgments   xiii

Chapter 1
INTRODUCTION   1

Chapter 2
DISCOVERY, DESIRE, AND DESTRUCTION:
EAST MEETS WEST   7

Chapter 3
SONGS OF DESIRE:
ENCOUNTERS THROUGH CRUSADE   19

Chapter 4
NEW SONGS WITH NEW RHYTHMS:
THE ROMANCE EPIC   35

Chapter 5
FORGING RELATIONSHIPS:
LAW, "HISTORY," AND NATIONAL IDENTITY   53

Chapter 6
QUESTIONING THE MYTH:
OBSTACLE AND REJECTION   67

Chapter 7
TRANSITIONAL FIGURES   83

Chapter 8
CONCLUSIONS   101

Figures   104
Bibliography   107
Index   117

ACKNOWLEDGMENTS

I wish to thank Per Nykrog and Jan Ziolkowski for their advice and suggestions in every stage of this project. Their help with sources, translations, and letter-writing for grants was invaluable and always highly appreciated. Sahar Amer has provided inspiration through her own work and enthusiasm for my interest in "things Saracen." Jann Matlock's moral support and ideas for theoretical directions have helped me throughout the years. María Rosa Menocal lent direction and encouragement. Travel grants from the Harvard University Graduate Society and the Lurcy Foundation allowed me access to primary sources in France at critical points during my research.

I also thank Frank Gentry for including my work in this series, Damon Zucca and Becca Murphy at Routledge for editing support, and my colleague John McCaw for his suggestions on clandestine research.

Most importantly, I am indebted to my family: to my parents for financial support and encouragement, to my husband who truly understood, and to my daughter for giving me incentive.

1. Introduction

The study of medieval French literature has been linked from its inception in the late-nineteenth century to nation formation and identity. During the Franco-Prussian War, Gaston Paris used the *Chanson de Roland*, calling it the "voice of the nation," to urge his students to follow the example of those who died at Roncevaux protecting their lands. One of those students, Joseph Bédier, took Paris' thesis one step further, referring to the *Chanson de Roland* as a lesson in national unity.[1] As France's first epic and first long work of literature, the *Roland* embodies in French literary history both the beginning of French literature and the beginning of the French nation. Indeed, the entire literary corpus of the French Middle Ages serves as a début, giving to a reader centuries removed from the period an introduction to all genres of French literature. The first known poem thus becomes the birth of French poetry, the first play the nascence of French theater, and so on.

Likewise, the ideas found in the literary texts of the period serve as one of our earliest introductions to French culture and imagination. The social and political fabric of what is now called France changed radically from 1100 to 1500, the time frame of almost all French literature categorized as "medieval." Lumped together as one period for study, the centuries that make up the Middle Ages in France are as varied as the 500 years of literary history that follow them. Vast strides were made in science and technology, much of the new knowledge imported from Arabic sources. Small, yet powerful, fiefdoms gave way to centralized government. Art and literature, inspired by many sources, saw a veritable explosion.

Early in the Middle Ages, national identity had no defined place. Those living in France, particularly former "barbarians," no doubt saw themselves as different from those in Rome. While tribal affiliations lingered, the people of Southern France aligned themselves more closely with those in Spain than those in Norman-dominated Northern France. Regionalism took precedence over nationalism, a concept that would come later in the Middle

Ages. Yet in many ways, the fracturing of regionalism led to a more open view of society. Regions were so small that their linguistic boundaries could not realistically provide sufficient resources for trade and social interaction. Travel of almost any distance brought new languages, ideas, and cultures into view. *Koiné*, or common language, developed, as found in the Provençal of the troubadours. Even religion was not all-encompassing; Christianity, plagued by heresies and division, still confronted paganism in the earlier years. At times during the Middle Ages, other religions, Judaism and Islam in particular, appeared to be more like alternative heresies than separate religions.

During this period, France began to define its borders, its language, its religion, and its values. Predictably, the model varied markedly over the centuries. That which was included in one model might well be excluded later. French took precedence over Occitan. The king dominated his barons and the independent houses of power in the South of France. The Muslim (then referred to as "Saracen") and the Jew were definitively rejected from French society. But these changes took place gradually, and over the years appear different visions of French society, before the lines between the races were so deeply drawn. The medieval French text offers a conflicted view, a look at a time when Self and Other were not so clearly defined and when Self and Other could actually trade places for a moment.

To better grasp the formation of the French "Self," this study looks into the role of the interethnic (French-Saracen) couple in medieval French literature. The term couple designates both same-sex and different-sex pairs. Not an exploration of love per se, though some of the couples are lovers, this study focuses on interpersonal relationships that are central to the text, be it lyric, epic, romance, or hybrid. These texts juxtapose the Self and the Other in fascinating ways in order to define cultural values. Determining meaning through juxaposition is far from unusual, as things are defined in relation to other things, either as same or as different. In nascent literatures, the focus on definition emerges especially forcefully, as all distinction becomes unique (there are no other literary models) and therefore totalizing. Changes in definitions can later subvert the older, unique model. As definitions multiply, multiplicity rather than exclusiveness results, but that multiplicity can occur only when a critical mass of texts has been written and, later, uncovered.

The modern world shares some dynamics of the Middle Ages. Nascent written literatures must struggle with the same concerns, whatever the time or place. As written voices emerge from cultures previously without written texts, the struggle for definition asserts itself. Thus the medieval European text has much in common with both colonial and post-colonial literatures. Like colonialist authors, medieval French writers employ the image of the Other (most often the Saracen in the Middle Ages) as a central part of their mission. While in both modern and medieval examples, the pleasure of the text is often the main issue, the method that the author uses to attract the reader can involve both denigration and exaltation of the Other. However, the post-colonial text also shares attributes of the medieval text. Just as the post-colonial writer often writes in a language imposed from without, so the medieval writer first expressed thoughts in Latin, then a Latin-hybrid, and, finally, in the Latin-based, ever-evolving language of a particular region. The use of koiné continued throughout the Middle Ages, as writers wrote in languages that were not their mother tongues, such as Provençal and, as always, Latin.

While it may seem contradictory to envision the literature of the French Middle Ages as similar to the writing of both the colonizer and the (post)colonized, medieval France shared many concerns of both groups. Contrary to the ancients, and even the Arabs in the High Middle Ages, France was only beginning to develop its national literature. The Bible, central to the culture of the time, was not even available in French. Closely linked to the growth of vernacular literature was the need to define the cultural models and write the histories for the emerging nation-states.

The link between nation and narration has been explored, if not in complete agreement by any of the parties, for the post-colonial novel by writers including Homi Bhabha and Frantz Fanon, and for the medieval epic by Gabrielle Spiegel. The view toward nationalism necessarily involves defining the groups to be included and excluded from the nation. Studies of the Other as a literary tool to nascent national literature have been far more examined by post-colonial critics than by medieval literature critics. To this point, studies of medieval literature have tended to isolate the Other as a theme or image in Western literature, without examining the implications of the representation of the Other to the audience of the texts. The role of the Saracen Other in medieval French literature, then, must take into account the personal or collective ends for which the Other was introduced in the first place.

The Saracen is often (though not always) seen as the complete opposite of the Christian, Western, French self: to say "Saracen" is in essence to say "evil." Saracens lose all ability to function as individuals. Their actions are pre-programmed by their "saracenness." In these texts, while the Christian is valiant and white as snow, for example, the Saracen will be cowardly and black as coal. Colonial texts may pick other pairs of opposites, but the effect is the same. As in André Gide's L'Immoraliste, the Other can represent the sensuality of which the European is devoid. Edward Said's study of Orientalism exposes some of the dichotomies forced upon the Other in the literature of the colonizer, particularly that of sexualized object in nineteenth-century travel literature. Negative views of the Saracen produced by the equation of good versus evil have been most popular among studies of the medieval Other. Norman Daniel's *Heroes and Saracens* and *Islam and the West: The Making of an Image* and Philippe Sénac's *L'image de l'autre* have as their starting point this fixed opposition between Self and Other.

Contrary to the common argument, the portraits of Saracens that emerge from the writings of the Middle Ages are conflicting and ambiguous. Some are condemning and completely negative while others show admiration or even desire. The same Saracen who might be chastised for his idolatry might be lauded as an exemplary knight. A Saracen woman, despite her association with the "wrong side," could equally well be the most resourceful character in a story and end up married to a Frenchman. In addition, and perhaps related to, the misperception that Saracens were equated only with evil and darkness in medieval French texts, many studies overlook a vast body of sources. Much work on medieval attitudes toward Islam neglects literary sources, preferring historical texts, ecclesiastical writing, and sermons. When literary sources are considered, frequently epic alone is examined. The epic is the genre of battle and has inherent limitations for considering social interaction. In the masculine world of the epic, the role of the male-female relationship is often minimized or omitted.

For the purposes of this analysis, as representations of the Saracen are examined throughout medieval French literature, they are not set apart from their *milieu*, but instead are grounded in their historical and cultural environment. Four main questions form the framework for this study. The first regards the relation between literary portraits of the Saracen and historical relationships between Saracen and Christian at the time the texts were produced. Are the Saracens in the text purely fictional, or do they represent to some degree a lived experience on the part of medieval authors or their *milieux*? In other words, how does the historical affect the imagination? Secondly, to what extent does the Saracen in the literary work function as an impetus to self-definition? Outsiders are often used as a point of departure, a method for defining the group that remains on the "inside." The medieval literary Muslim often played this role, serving as foil for the Christian community. Conversion and integration of the Muslim reinforce the priorities of European society. Likewise, exclusion and execution serve to draw lines of difference between the two societies, putting one side clearly in the right and the other in the wrong. My third question directly addresses the lacuna in many studies of the Saracen Other. What difference does gender make? In certain cases, the Saracen Other is clearly treated differently depending on the gender of the person. How does gender serve to create or efface difference between the Other and the Self? Does the treatment of the Saracen Other reinforce Lacan's notion that the basic binary is that of male/female rather than what some might call a medieval perspective of Christian/Saracen, or do race and religion trump gender? My final line of inquiry is the parallel between the literary and the non-literary tradition. Writings by clerics, sermons and non-literary texts such as law-books also treat the Saracen Other and his or her relationship to the European Christian. What is the relationship between these different and yet simultaneous discourses? In what ways do they inform each other while each one reflecting a certain aspect of the relationship between Self and Other?

In studying the conflicting views of Muslims that are found in literary couples, one finds a gradual change in the image of the Other that corresponds roughly to the changing cultural climate. The first impulse is one of discovery, desire, and destruction. Initial contact with Saracens opened a new world of refinement and luxury to the medieval European. Even as authors wished to possess the material wealth of the Saracens, they rejected the religion and customs of the Muslim. A desire for what is far away and different is reflected in the lyric poetry of Provençal poets who abstracted the Orient and Arab women and made absence the locus of desire. Early chansons de geste like *Gormont et Isembart* and the *Chanson de Roland* portray a Saracen enemy who is not without admirable traits. Nonetheless, the final goal is total destruction of the Other, with attempts at integration being non-existent. In the *Chanson de Roland*, however, the role of gender is made apparent as one conversion is possible—that of Bramimonde, the wife of the conquered enemy.

The second major wave of stories depicting Muslim/Christian interaction were the chansons de geste, where Christians began to see the Muslims as ever-present elements of their world. Fighting had failed to expel the Muslims, so Christians had to create laws, structures, and rules for coping (both economically and socially) with their Muslim neighbors. Laws regarding intermarriage cropped up at the same time that literary images of the interracial couple proliferated. The topos of the Saracen princess who aids French crusaders is found in at least 17 different chansons de geste. Orable, Saracen wife of Guillaume d'Orange, steals the show in the *Prise d'Orange*, where she saves the French crusaders and orchestrates her marriage to Guillaume. Laws and rules were one way of coping with a now-internal Other; literature provided another outlet for social anxiety.

The period of the chanson de geste was followed by a questioning of the model of cohabitation that had been developed in the 12th and 13th centuries. The concept of harmony began to crumble as parody and nostalgia dominated literary treatment of the Muslim/Christian couple. Whereas Orable and Guillaume could marry without societal objection, *Aucassin et Nicolette* and *Floire et Blancheflor* are two examples of tales where intense pressure is put on the interethnic couple to prevent intermarriage. Over the centuries, different versions of the *Fille du comte de Ponthieu* star a French heroine who progressively rejects her adopted Saracen family more and more definitively. Time proves unkind to the Saracen-Christian relationship.

The changes that took place on a thematic level translated into changes on a structural level. As relationships between Christian and Saracen changed, writers found that older ways of writing could not adequately construct and question the evolving social situation. Epic serves well to talk of societies in conflict but, try as it might, cannot express longing and desire as well as lyric. The romance epic, given a hybrid appellation precisely because it did not fit into received notions of genre, makes perfect sense as a hybrid genre, acknowledging conflict while simultaneously expressing possibilities of alliance. Other mixed-genre texts, including the infamous hybrid *Aucassin et Nicolette*, function as markers of social and literary confusion. While older, epic models did not quite capture the Christian-Saracen relationship, neither could authors accept a completely romanticized view of cohabitation. As occurred frequently in medieval historiography, the line between history and fiction blurred when describing Christian-Saracen interactions. Law code contained scenarios highly reminiscent of epic romance, while epic romance mirrored or even fabricated Christian-Muslim romance at the highest social levels. Prester John, created as a ploy to unify Europe, lost his fictional status when explorers claimed to find his kingdom. Generic conventions from epic to lyric to romance to history to law could not contain or describe the Christian-Saracen relationship, and the new genres demanded by the ever-changing roles correspond to generic French literary history. Hans Robert Jauss claims, "The theory of literary genres cannot remain within the structures of the self-enclosed histories of genres, but rather must also consider the possibility of a historical systematics."[2] The importance of the Christian-Saracen relationship to French literature is underscored, not only on the level of influence (or borrowing), but even more so because the very notion of literary form had to change in an always-futile attempt to fully describe a social "problem" that dominated medieval Europe from 1100–1500.

The use of literary models for establishing patterns of social interaction is imperative for understanding the European Middle Ages. The line between history and fiction was intentionally blurred, as Gabrielle Spiegel's work on historiography and epic has shown. The complex relationship between France and the Middle East that exists today has a history stretching back before the Crusades. In re-reading the Christian-Muslim relationship portrayed in medieval French literature in light of historical and cultural referents, perhaps we can better grasp not simply the origins of Orientalism, but also the essential role of conflict to the origins of French literary history.

NOTES

1. Joseph Bédier, *Les legendes épiques*, 3rd ed. (Paris: Champion, 1926–29), vol. 3, p. 452. For an excellent overview of the Paris and Bédier theses and their impact on medieval studies, see R. Howard Bloch, "842. The First Document and the Birth of Medieval Studies," in *A New History of French Literature*, ed. D. Hollier (Cambridge: Harvard University Press, 1989), pp. 6–13.

2. Hans Robert Jauss, "Genres and Medieval Literature," *Toward an Aesthetic of Reception*, trans. Timothy Bahti (Minneapolis: University of Minnesota Press, 1982), p. 95. See also "Literary History as a Challenge to Literary Theory" in the same volume.

2. Discovery, Desire, and Destruction: East Meets West

Islam and Arabic came to the West on a tide of violence and destruction. In the thirteenth century the monks of the abbey of Vézelay chronicled earlier Saracen raids into Provence:

> The barbarian nation having attacked the city of Aix, and having taken it, pillaged it completely, taking a large number of prisoners. All the others perished by sword and by fire. They burned alive many men and women, as the Saracens have the custom of doing to our people, and as we have since seen. After this disaster, that we believe to be the punishment for the sins of these people (the inhabitants of Aix), they soon returned to their lands.[1]

These first images of the Saracen as bringer of death and destruction lingered in the portrayal of the Saracen in medieval French literature. Although Charles Martel halted the northern progression of raids into France in the eighth century, the violence of the seventh and eighth centuries left its mark on the French cultural imagination.

The oldest known epic in France, the *Chanson de Roland*, which dates from around 1100, bears the traces of battles that had taken place about 200 years earlier. While ostensibly telling the story of Charlemagne at Roncevaux in 778, the events of the *Chanson de Roland* have been shifted into a contemporary setting, superimposing a long history of concerns about the Muslim upon the palpable fear of Muslim invasion that gripped France in Charles Martel's and Charlemagne's time. The historical basis of the battle, most likely a decimation of Charlemagne's rear guard in 778 by Basques then in control of the mountains separating present-day France and Spain, is transformed to make it more understandable, even more tragic, for the early twelfth-century audience. The Basques should have been allies of Charlemagne in his fight against the Muslim invaders. Charlemagne, however, apparently treated the Basques with hostility on his way down into

Spain, and on his return was greeted with angry forces. The eleventh-century epic changes the enemy of the tale to fit in with contemporary expectations. Basques were not the evil enemy anymore, nor in fact were they ever. In the historical version, Charlemagne shares responsibility for the slaughter of his troops due to his rough treatment of potential allies. The tale of Christian versus Saracen makes a much better contrast between right and wrong. Charlemagne's struggle with the Saracen forces takes on the guise of good versus evil, right versus wrong, that makes ideal material for an epic tragedy.

In the early twelfth century concrete knowledge about the customs, habits and religion of the Muslims was little or non-existent. One of the problems when dealing with these invasions is precisely what to call the peoples who invaded Spain and the south of France. While the impetus certainly came from the extraordinary success of the followers of Muhammad, the people who actually carried out the invasions were not homogenous. Having come via Morocco and the Straits of Gibraltar up through Spain, the invaders included Muslim Arabs, as well as a strong contingent of Berber tribesmen who had not yet converted to Islam.[2] The victorious group did not even speak the same language, some conversing in Berber and others in Arabic. In many ways then, the medieval term of Saracen to refer to this disparate group of peoples embodies a generalizing and therefore more accurate terminology appropriate for the period.

The term Saracen is probably derived from the Greek, sarakenos[3], the word used to describe the Arab invaders following the precepts of Muhammad. According to Godefroy, sarasin, sarrazin refers to the entire Orient, the land of the Saracens. Linguistic confusion reigned, however, as writers clearly did not see the Saracens as a particular group of people with unique customs and beliefs. The term Saracen could thus be used to describe enemies residing in Hungary or the Holy Land, and even the Normans, with apparently no need for justification on the part of the author of a text. Thus Saracen can be interpreted as "pagan," a word that is used interchangeably with "Saracen" to describe a valiant warrior. In the late Middle Ages, the remains of Roman architecture, long-since unused and of forgotten origin, were sometimes called Saracen, as Godefroy notes, "sarasinois—appliqué a un ouvrage de construction il indiquait des ruines romaines." At its essence, the term "Saracen" seems to hold the same place in the medieval imagination that "foreign," "exotic," or "outlandish" represents for us.

This study is focused on the historical and imagined interactions between Christians and Muslims in France in the Middle Ages. The linguistic confusion resulting from the many uses of the term Saracen is of inherent interest to such a project; in what ways did the French imagination see Hungarians and Andalusian Muslims as similar enough to call them by the same name? It would indeed be impossible to know what the medieval author was imagining as he or she used the term "Saracen" to denote very different groups of people. Nonetheless, for the vast majority of the cases, spread throughout the centuries, the word "Saracen" referred to Arabic-speaking, Muslim peoples.

The linguistic fluidity of the word *Saracen* fits well with the variations in eponymous portraits. One of the most intriguing and appealing elements of medieval views of the Other is the tendency to vacillate between the oppositional and the similar. Even within the same text, one Saracen may be the ultimate coward or the most hideous of all apostates, while another may be beautiful, noble, and/or valiant, lacking only a faith in the true God to attain perfection. The Saracen functions on multiple levels in and among texts, sometimes acting as a negative foil to the Christian hero and other times distinguishing himself or herself by extraordinary activities.

The *Chanson de Roland* is a text that undoubtedly speaks of the Saracen as Muslim, yet understanding of Islam plays no role in the text. In a piece of propaganda such as this chanson de geste one would not necessarily expect the author to take a great interest in truthfully exposing the tenets of Islam and the differences with Christianity[5]. However, even the basic elements of the religion are lacking. The poet credits the infidels with numerous gods, contrary to the monotheism that makes "There is no god but God" the first and most fundamental belief of Islam. Examples of this misunderstanding include: "Li reis Marsilie la tient, ki Deu nen aimet ; Mahumet sert e Apollin recleimet."[6] |King Marsilie who does not love God holds Saragossa; he serves Muhammad and calls on Apollin.|

When the Saracens swear an oath to do their best to kill Roland, they do so on their holy book, mistaking Muhammad and Tervagant as the authors of, presumably, the Koran, whereas Islam holds the book to be the literal word of God: "Marsilies fait porter un livre avant :/ La lei i fut Mahum e Tervagan."[7] |Marsilie had a book brought forth: In it was the law of Muhammad and Tervagant.| The Saracens, anticipating the return and vengeance of Charlemagne, pray to one of their gods, Tervagant,[8] who predictably does not come to their aid. Angry at the non-response of their gods, the Saracens[9] desecrate their own temple, cursing and tearing down the statues to Tervagant, Muhammad and Apollin. This scene reflects perhaps the ultimate sacrilege to the Christian community, which believed quite strongly in icons, but it makes no sense in Islam as images and pictorial representations were and are not permitted.

The Saracen warrior mirrors the Christian quite frequently throughout the text. Charlemagne retires to an orchard, underneath a pine tree, following his initial defeat of the Saracens. Here his 15,000 soldiers gather around, but most notably present are the pairs, Charlemagne's closest men and advisors with whom he proceeds to discuss plans for leaving Spain.[10] Marsile, the Arab ruler, also goes into an orchard following the same battle and is described as sitting in the shade. His 20,000 men surround him, and he takes this moment to call his closest advisors (called here "dux" et "cuntes") to brainstorm on how to finally crush the French.[11] The political and governing strategies of the two groups are the same. Both leaders are greatly respected by their men, yet their best ideas and future directions come from a select group of noble advisors (dukes and counts), many of whom are related to each other and to the king. As Marsile and his men seal their treachery, the parallelism is complete; twelve chosen from the Saracens, led by the nephew of Marsile, will go head to head with the twelve companions of Charlemagne, led by Roland, his nephew:

> Li niés Marsilies tient le guant en sun poign,
> Eslisez mei .XII. de voz baruns,
> Sim cumbatrai as .XII. cumpaignuns.[12]

> [The nephew of Marsile held the glove in his fist,
> Choose for me 12 of your barons,
> and so I will combat the 12 companions.]

The glove that the Saracen carries as representative of his ruler will be the same emblem that Ganelon, ambassador of Charlemagne, will accept from his king.

The Saracen doubles the Christian in other aspects of the epic as well. During the battle, as is the convention in most battle scenes of the chansons de geste, each Christian knight meets individually with a Saracen knight. Blows are exchanged and one knight emerges victorious, having killed the other. The two armies are equipped identically, though a certain exoticism dominates the description of the Saracen outfit:

> Paien s'adubent des osbercs sarazineis,
> Tuit li plusur en sunt dublez en treis.
> Lacent lor elmes mult bons sarraguzeis,
> Ceignent espees de l'acer vianeis ;
> Escuz unt genz, espiez valentineis,
> E gunfanuns blancs e blois e vermeilz.
> Laissent les mulz e tuz les palefreiz,
> Es destrers muntent, si chevalchent estreiz.[13]

> [The pagans armed themselves with Saracen hauberks of which most were lined with three thicknesses. They laced their very good helmets from Saragossa and cinched their swords of Venetian steel. They carried beautiful shields, pikes from Valencia, and white, blue, and green standards. They left aside their mules and palfreys and mounted on their war-horses, riding in tight lines.]

The armor remains essentially western, as do the basic riding techniques (on a special war-horse, in tight lines). Yet, the Saracen *is* distinguished from the French by the provenance of his "sarazineis" weaponry. The author gives the impression that excellent, perhaps the best, armor comes from far away, from the pagan lands of Saragossa and Valencia, in addition to Venice. No doubt about it, the Saracen is regally equipped. The shield of an Emir holds equal fascination and beauty, "Pierres i ad, amestistes e topazes,

Esterminals e carbuncles ki ardent.¹⁴" [It was encrusted in stones, amethysts, topazes, diamonds, and gleaming carbuncles.]

Admiration for the Saracen is not limited to his armor. The Saracen knight can be noble, handsome, loyal and bold. In short, all the same characteristics admired in the Christian knight can be found in certain Saracen knights as well. The author highlights the prowess and beauty of the Saracen Margarit: "Margariz est mult vaillant chevalers, / E bels e forz e isnels e legers.¹⁵" [Margarit is a valiant knight, handsome, fast, and lively.] The Emir of Balaguer serves as a prime example of the knight who would be perfect, were he only a Christian:

> Uns amurafles i ad de Balaguez :
> Cors ad mult gent e le vis fier e cler ;
> Puis que il est sur sun cheval muntet,
> Mult se fait fiers de ses armes porter ;
> De vasselage est il ben alosez ;
> Fust chrestiens, asez oüst barnet.¹⁶

[There was an Emir from Balaguer, well-fashioned body and a proud and light face. When he had gotten on his horse, he was well distinguished in carrying arms. He is well known to be a good vassal. If he were Christian, he would be a true baron.]

Physically, even, this Saracen shares the traits of the Christian. His skin, most noticeably, is white.

Abdul R. JanMohamed's inquiry into the economy of the manichean allegory in colonialist literature offers a revealing framework for understanding the medieval Other.¹⁷ Inspired by the work of Jacques Lacan, he divides colonialist literature into types, the "imaginary" and the "symbolic." The "imaginary" novel looks to the indigenous people as dangerous and evil: a negative force that must be controlled. In this kind of novel the Manichean allegory has rule, setting up the native and the self as non-overlapping opposites. The drive to exterminate the Other is paramount, as descriptions of mutilated bodies abound. Natural or genetic categories replace socially or ideologically determined ones. The native can be nothing other than what he or she is because of some inherent property of the race. The native is fetishized, no longer subject to circumstance, intention, or causality. The signifier becomes the signified.

The "symbolic" novel is willing to admit of a non-manichean relationship between the European and the native. The Other allows for an examination of Self. The contrast between the different cultures can highlight negative or questionable aspects of the writer's own culture. These novels permit a flexible view of both European and native. The native may remain Other, but the Other is not predetermined. A sense of ambivalence replaces the automatic judgment of his or her actions. Those novels which examine the imaginary, looking at the process by which colonialist mentality inevitably constructs the Other as overdetermined, free themselves completely from the manichean allegory.

Needless to say, differences abound between post-colonial or colonial literature and medieval French literature. Nonetheless, the medieval writer also wrestled with representations of the cultural Other. The historical becomes of evident importance when contextualizing the medieval representation of the Saracen, distinguishing it from the colonial experience. The Muslim invasions of Spain and even France in the eighth century thrust Western Europeans into uncomfortably close contact with another culture and religion. Christians and Muslims remained enemies on the battlefield for another 700 years, but their rapport changed significantly during this period. Whereas early fighting focused mainly on stemming the seemingly endless flood of invaders into Christian lands, not long after the time of Charles Martel the lines were fairly firmly fixed. Those lands under permanent occupation by Saracens were always coveted, but the threat of loss of further life and property had diminished. The dream of Reconquest was everpresent, however, and forays into Spain to capture Muslim towns were not uncommon from the eleventh century onward. While this cultural contact was hostile by definition, other practical relationships had begun to form and would continue to flourish until the end of the Reconquest in 1492. Trading relationships, ambassadorial envoys and even cohabitation exposed authors north of the Pyrenees to a culture, language and religion quite different from their own.

The author's capacity to note the positive in the Saracen knight marks the text's participation in the realm of the "symbolic," as described by JanMohamed. The author is able to step back from the dichotomy of good versus evil that forms the basis of the epic in order to admit a certain similitude and even admiration. The armor of the Christian knights is not quite so fabulous as that of the Saracen. The Emir of Balaguer distinguishes himself as almost a true baron, to be compared with the treasonous Ganelon. By bringing the two armies together in moments of similarity, an implicit examination of the values and culture of the Christian results. Better weaponry can be found in other cultures. Superior knights are not limited to the French, and indeed certain Christian knights fall short of their Saracen counterparts.

The Saracen is not without his abominable traits, however. Roland sees the approaching hordes through a literal perspective of black versus white:

> ... Rollant veit la contredite gent
> Ki plus sunt neirs que nen est arrement,
> Ne n'unt de blanc ne mais que sul les denz....[18]
>
> [Roland saw the accursed people, who are blacker than ink and have no white except for their teeth alone.]

The essentialism of the "imaginary" text demands that the entire race be not only accursed, but also of a uniform and total blackness. Their white teeth, comically, served only to contrast and heighten their utter darkness.

Just as the Emir of Balaguer epitomized the almost-ideal knight, the appropriately named Saracen, Abyss, serves as the stereotypical concentration of the fears of the Other.

> Devant chevalchet un sarrasin, Abisme :
> Plus fel de lui n'out en sa cumpagnie.
> Te(t)ches ad males e mult granz felonies ;
> Ne creit en Deu, le filz sainte Marie ;
> Issi est neirs cume peiz ki est demise ;
> Plus aimet il traïsun e murdrie
> Qu'(e) il fesist trestut l'or de Galice ;
> Unches nuls hom nel vit juer ne rire.[19]

[Out in front rode a Saracen, Abyss. There was none more treacherous in his following. He is charged with evils and very great villainies. He does not believe in God, the son of Saint Mary. He is as dark as molten pitch, and he loves treason and murder better than all the gold of Galicia. No person had ever seen him play or laugh.]

Not only is Abyss morally corrupt, he is also physically repulsive. His very humanness is called into question by his inability or unwillingness to laugh and play. As the fears of the Other are essentialized and fetishized in the figure of Abyss, the impulse to destroy the evil Other surges at its strongest. Turpin, the archbishop/knight, takes it upon himself to destroy the personified evil. As he kills Abyss, the French are moved to call out Turpin's praises: " Ci ad grant vasselage! / En l'arcevesque est ben la croce salve."[20] [What a valiant vassal! With the archbishop, the honor of the cross is safe.] The manichean dichotomy emerges; the fight is nothing other than good versus evil, right versus wrong, truth versus lies.

The story of *Gormont and Isembart*[21] tells of the tragic intertwining of two lives, one Christian and one Saracen. Like the *Chanson de Roland*, this epic changes the account of a historical battle, pitting East against West, rather than French versus Norman. Many attempts have been made to determine exactly which battle was the basis for this 661-line fragment of a chanson de geste. All that can be definitively said about the fragment is that it follows the standard epic plot line, with individual battles being waged between strong warriors from both sides. In the end, as is so often true, the only person who can defeat the pagan king is the French king, and he can succeed in his quest only with divine intervention. Efforts to find a historical basis for this event seem rather pointless as the events could describe any battle at any time during the French Middle Ages. Such historical readings of the chanson de geste probably indicate more about the late nineteenth-century drive to establish medieval literature as an important, historical discipline rather than any real understanding of the medieval author's desire to create and entertain. Nonetheless, critical inquiry has seemed to settle on the battle of Saucourt in 881 between Louis III and the Normans, led by a renegade named Turmon.[22]

The text tells a different story. The pagan king, Gormond, is twice said to be from the Orient, "celui d'Oriente"[23], "cist d'Oriante".[24] He is also called "li Arabi"[25], and like his brothers in the *Chanson de Roland*, he swears by the god Apollin.[26] His men are referred to as "Sarrazins"[27] as well as "Turz e Persanz e Arabiz".[28] The geste, like the *Chanson de Roland*, shows no understanding of Muslim culture or religion, and the geography of the epic makes little sense to a real historical understanding of a fight between Christians and Muslims (for instance, once defeated, Gormont's troops flee to the North rather than the South or East). Nonetheless, the author has unquestionably invoked the Saracen: the Muslim (follower of Apollin) and Arab (Arabi) Saracen. No matter what the historical battle may have been, the ever-present, ultimate enemy for the twelfth century continued to be the Muslim.

Even as the Muslim is the ultimate enemy, he is not without admirable qualities. Gormond offers an especially clear case of the medieval ambivalence toward the Muslim. While his status as an unbeliever made him unredeemable—he is once called the Antichrist[29]—Gormond embodies the medieval ideal of the valiant warrior. The text makes plain his worthiness:

> Li meudre rei e le plus franc
> qui unques fust el munde vivant,
> se il creust Deu le poant . . .[30]

> [He was the best king and the most noble living in the world if only he believed in God the powerful]

Gormond defeats handily all of the best knights the French king has to send his way. King Louis himself, if not for the aid of God, would have fallen to the Saracen knight.[31] Indeed, the French king is said not to last beyond 30 days after killing Gormond due to injuries sustained by the stress of the fight.[32]

Another example of the "symbolic" image of the Saracen, the admiration for Gormond indicates of the medieval admiration for the East. By the twelfth century, reports from the courts of Andalusia and travelers to Muslim lands made plain the advanced nature of Muslim civilization. It would be difficult for the French to picture the Arab as an uncouth barbarian. But the epic is the genre of battle, lending itself perfectly to the juxtaposition between good and evil. The Arab must always eventually fall to Christian; if not, where would that leave God and his power to intercede on behalf of his own? It could be said that the strength and might of the Saracen enemy only served to illustrate further the power of the French. However, this interpretation does not account for two facts. The power of the French is hardly heightened in this account as the Saracen defeats all the best French warriors, except when God intercedes. Even more importantly, the medieval fascination with the invincible knight gives prime status to the successful warrior. In a culture where trial by combat meant that "might makes right," the successful warrior had the most enviable social position. God enabled the just warrior to defeat those who were in the wrong. Isembart, the French renegade who joins forces with the Saracens, represents the fascination and homosocial attraction between the French and the Saracen. While Isembart's desire to please the strong pagan king is seen as misguided, the praises heaped on Gormond by the text explain that attraction and desire. The author paints Gormond as a much more attractive figure, being kinder and more generous, than his French counterpart, Louis, and this sentiment echoes through the chronicles and stories surrounding the epic. The Anonymous of Béthune, writing after the geste, specifies that "Looys se fist molt haïr a plusiors."[33] Thus the Saracen could be rich, generous, kind, and an excellent warrior. This model of the ideal ruler for the Middle Ages contrasts sharply with some images of Christian rulers. Like Louis, Marie de France's Arthur in "Lanval" pales in comparison with Gormond. Arthur's neglect of his troops, particularly Lanval, shows a basic character flaw in the king. The generosity of the ruler supplies the basis for his soldiers' existence, and Arthur fails on this fundamental level to provide for Lanval's needs. This action in turn motivates the story of the fantastic, otherwordly sponsor who gives Lanval what his own leader should have. The Saracen Gormond operates in the same otherworldly realm as Lanval's fairy queen, both functioning as implicit criticisms of a specific element or problem in medieval French society, namely the forgetful or stingy lord.

The impulse to go over to the Saracen camp, as Isembart did, equals the drive to annihilate this most potent of enemies. The desire that leads to following the Saracen leader furnishes the momentum for his eventual demise. One may wish to be like the Saracen, but this very attraction necessitates his removal. The Saracen threatens most when he is virtually flawless.

The Saracen participates in both the symbolic and the imaginary, sometimes even within the same text. The hybrid text offers the author a mode of both including and excluding the Saracen. The author admires certain traits of the Saracen, thus encouraging acceptance of the Saracen Other in readers/listeners of his culture. At the same time, by offering stereotypical formulations of the evil Saracen, the author unites himself with his own people against the Other. This pushing and pulling at the image of the Saracen finally breaks down all efforts to categorize the Other. How can he be both ultimately admirable and the epitome of what is abominable, as is the case with Gormond? The Saracen as person disappears from the text and becomes an empty signifier that the author can use to denote whatever he or she wishes. In the case of Gormond, the Saracen character serves only to highlight Isembart's inner conflict. Should he remain loyal to a bad king (Louis), or does he have a right to fight for a more worthy leader?

Learning that a character is a Saracen adds nothing to the reader/listener's understanding of the text until the author elaborates exactly to what kind of Saracen he or she is referring. This provides the hybrid text, one that includes both positive and negative images of the Saracen, an opportunity to break away from the accepted and the anticipated. The author is free to create his or her Saracen as needed for the text; Gormond and Baligant may embody the good knight. This phenomenon is especially true when the same Saracen has positive and negative traits, but the dialectic forces in a text that provides both positive and negative images can also accomplish the same goal.

The freedom of the medieval epic author to reinscribe at each instance the meaning of "Saracen" does not translate to cultural acceptance, however. The Saracen, when detested, unites the French against the Other. The admirable Saracen serves to criticize basic structures of French society. While criticizing, authors of medieval epic do not advocate destruction of their own society. In the final analysis, the French will triumph over the Saracen, no matter how superior the latter may prove himself in battle.

The goal of the epic is to create unity, whether through opposition with the Other, thus reinforcing national identity, or by highlighting a shared cultural experience, such as suffering at the hands of an inept or evil ruler. The epic can only allow for certain hierarchical relationships[34] where Christian and Muslim societies mirror each other. Epic authors hold up the comparison to correct and not subvert their own society. In addition, characterization is constrained by the epic genre. The static nature of the epic center (the courts of Charlemagne or Louis) does not allow for individuation.[35] Clearly, then, for the medieval author to depict other relationships between Christian and Muslim, epic as previously defined no longer fits the bill, and new genres will need to be employed.

NOTES

1. Philippe Sénac, L'*image de l'autre: histoire de l'occident médiéval face à Islam* (Paris: Flammarion, 1983), 24. Sénac quotes from the thirteenth-century chronicle of the monks of Vézelay. See also G. de Rey, *Les Invasions des Sarrasins en Provence*, (Marseille, 1971), p. 147 and Charles Melville and Ahmad Ubaydli, *Christians and Moors in Spain: Volume III Arabic Sources* (711–1501)(Warminster, England: Aris & Phillips, 1992) for more reports of this sort.

2. Richard Fletcher, *Moorish Spain* (London: Weidenfeld & Nicolson, 1992), 19–20.

3. Sénac, op. cit., p. 14.

4. Philippe Lauer, "Louis IV d'Outre-mer et le fragment d'Isembart et Gormont." *Romania* 26 (1897), pp. 161–74; Lauer notes a few examples of naming non-Arabs as "saracen." In Wace's *Roman de Rou* (423) and the *Roman d'Aquin ou la conqueste de la Bretaigne* (58, 447, etc.) the Normans receive the title of Saracen. Likewise, the Hungarians in the geste of the *Lorrains* and the Slavs in *Baligant* are so named.

Discovery, Desire, and Destruction: East Meets West 17

5. For a provocative look at the propagandic element of the geste, see the excellent article by Hans E. Keller, "The Song of Roland : a Mid-Twelfth Century Song of Propaganda for the Capetian Kingdom," *Olifant* 3 (1975–76): 242–58.
6. *La Chanson de Roland*, ed. Joseph Bédier (Paris: Union Générale d'Éditions, 1982), lines 7–8.
7. Ibid., lines 610–11.
8. Ibid., line 2468.
9. Ibid., lines 2587–91.
10. Ibid., lines 103–9.
11. Ibid., lines 10–24.
12. Ibid., lines 874–78.
13. Ibid., lines 994–1001.
14. Ibid., lines 1500–1.
15. Ibid., lines 1311–12.
16. Ibid., lines 894–99.
17. Abdul R. JanMohamed, "The Economy of Manichean Allegory: The Function of Racial Difference in Colonialist Literature." *Critical Inquiry* 12(1) (1985), pp. 59–87.
18. Roland, op. cit., lines 1932–34.
19. Ibid., lines 1470–77.
20. Ibid., lines 1508–09.
21. The dating of *Gormond et Isembart* has been contested in many different studies, but the findings of Gaston Paris (*Romania* 31 (1902), pp. 445–6) are quite convincing. He rejects based on historical circumstances the possibility that the chanson de geste could be as old as the eleventh century. The claim of King Louis in the poem to Saint-Denis could only come after 1082 when Philippe 1er became protector of Saint-Denis. Paris' remarks, taken in consideration with other considerable data attesting to the poem's early origins, would call for an early twelfth-century dating of the text.
22. Philippe Lauer, "Louis IV d'Outre-mer et le fragment d'Isembart et Gormont," *Romania* 26 (1897): 161–74. and Ferdinand Lot, "Gormond et Isembart: recherches sur les fondements historiques de cette épopée," *Romania* 27 (1898), pp. 1–54.
23. *Gormont et Isembart*, ed. Alphonse Bayot (Paris:Champion, 1931), line 69.
24. Ibid., line 78.
25. Ibid., lines 186, 443.
26. Ibid., line 193.
27. Ibid., lines 340, 448, 501, etc.
28. Ibid., line 433.
29. Ibid., line 204.
30. Ibid., lines 29–31.
31. Ibid., lines 386–87.
32. Ibid., lines 412–13.
33. As cited in Lauer, op. cit., p. 165.
34. Ollier notes, "La chanson de geste, c'est l'éclatante affirmation d'une com-

munauté qui se saisit comme telle; c'est l'irruption dans l'histoire d'une prise de conscience collective." See Marie-Louise Ollier, "Demande Sociale et Constitution d'un 'Genre': la situation dans la France du XIIe siecle," Mosaic 8 (4) (1975), p. 208–9.

35.   W. T. H. Jackson, "The Epic Center as Structural Determinant in Medieval Narrative Poetry," in The Challenge of the Medieval Text. ed. Joan M. Ferrante and Robert W. Hanning (NY: Columbia Unversity Press, 1985), p. 108.

3. Songs of Desire: Encounters Through Crusade

At the same time that the essentially male-centered epics focus on fear of the Saracen and the impulse to annihilate the enemy, the songs of the early troubadours indicate a different take on the Other. The songs of desire, inspired by women from afar and most probably even borrowing from Arabic poetry of the period[1], show profound ambivalence toward the Muslim neighbor. For even as the early Saracen invasions had left a bitter memory in the French consciousness, by the late eleventh and early twelfth century contact between Muslims and Christians had developed beyond the battlefield. The courts of Andalusia were flourishing in this period, and their prestige extended far beyond the borders of Spain. Some fortunate young Christian men sought out the Muslim schools in Spain to learn from the leading scholars of the time. Arab learning—philosophy and science, in particular—held a fascination for Christian scholars. The language of the courts and of much courtly literature in Spain was Arabic. While Spanish Christians had mixed with Muslim Andalusians for centuries, those north of the Pyrenees were just beginning to grasp the refinement, luxury, and sophistication of the Andalusian courts.

French Christians and Spanish Muslims interacted on many levels. Trade between the cultures conveyed some of the fabulous material wealth of the Muslims to courts in France. On a more somber note, the beginnings of the crusades into Spain brought foreign captives and slaves to the French. The story of one such invasion, the siege of Barbastro, is attested by both Muslim and Christian chroniclers. In 1064, a group of Norman Christians invaded Spain and besieged the Muslim-held city of Barbastro. After a reported siege of 40 days, the city fell to the Franco-Normans when the aqueduct feeding the city's water supply was fortuitously blocked by a catapult stone. The victors convinced the inhabitants of the highly-fortified city to surrender with promises that no one would be harmed. When the city was opened to the invaders, however, a general carnage followed. Contemporary historians do not agree on exact numbers, but estimates of 40,000 citizens slaughtered may not be exaggerated. Amatus of Monte Cassino writes of the capture in his 1080 *Historia Normannorum*. al-Bakri, a Muslim historian, also mentions the siege in his *al-Masalik wa'l-mamalik*:

> The people of Ghalish (Southern France) and the Normans raided [Barbastro] unexpectedly, due to its small number of defenders and their lack of readiness. . . . They besieged it for 40 days until they captured it. . . . They massacred the men and took a countless number of Muslim children and women as prisoners. It is related that they picked out 5,000 Muslim virgins and beauties and sent them as a present to the ruler of Constantinople.[2]

Another Muslim historian, Ibn Hayyan, writes:

> Le butin que les mécreants firent a Barbastro fut immense. Leur général en chef, le commandant de la cavalerie de Rome [Robert Crespin] eut pour sa part, dit-on, environ quinze cents jeunes filles et cinq cents charges de meuble, d'ornements, d'habits et de tapis. On raconte aussi qu'a cette occasion cinquante mille personnes furent réduites en captivité ou tuées.[3]

These reports indicate that large groups of Muslim women were led off in captivity, most likely to Rome, Constantinople and Southern France.

This huge influx (no matter how exaggerated the numbers might be, the relative importance of the quantity of captives is clear) of Arabic-speaking Muslims into France could not be without impact on nascent French literary culture. Indeed, the son of the man to whom the captives of Barbastro were given was no other than the first known troubadour, William, VII Count of Poitiers, IX Duke of Aquitaine. For his own part, William went on crusade in both Spain and the Holy Land, remaining in Jerusalem for several years during the time of "virtually complete acculturation of the crusaders to Arab ways."[4]

A master of language, William of Aquitaine addresses the uncertainty of speech in his poem *Farai un vers, pos me sonelh*. The poet garbs himself in pilgrim's clothing yet his later actions show that devotion is far from his first priority. The poet/pilgrim feigns ignorance of the women's language, noting that it is *"son* latin" (*her* language), not the poet's own language. In the verses cited below, the pilgrim understands the speech of the women, yet he comprehends a different message, namely that a lack of comprehension will actually serve him better. Thus he responds in a third language, neither his nor the women's, to convey his suitability for their purposes. The poem reads:

> la una.m diz en son latin :
> "E Dieus vos salf, don pelerin ;
> mout mi semblatz de bel aizin,
> Mon escient ;
> Mas trop vezem anar pel mon
> De folla gent. "

Ar auzires qu'ai respondut ;
Anc no li diz ni bat ni but,
Ni fer ni fust no ai mentaugut,
Mas sol aitan :
"Babariol, babariol,
Babarian."[5]

|One said to me in her language[6]: "God keep you, sir pilgrim; you seem to me to be from a very good place / but we see many fools going about in the world.
Now listen to how I responded to her; I didn't say "bat" nor "but" to her, I didn't speak to her of tools or of sleeves, but I said only this: "Babariol, babariol, Babarian." |

Believing the pilgrim to be unable to kiss and tell, the women proceed to make him a most willing sexual slave. In not speaking of tools or of sleeves, which have been interpreted as sexually related imagery,[7] the pilgrim accomplishes intercourse on a physical rather than verbal level. He remains master of the situation, for in fact he is the only party to understand all facets of their interaction.

The pilgrim's response, "babariol, babariol, babarian," has been read as everything from simple nonsense words to perverted Arabic. The relationship with *barbare*, or barbarian, is striking. William's application of this term is ambiguous. Is he referring to the pilgrim, and thus perhaps to himself, as well, or the women? In his macaronic declension of the word, he may well indicate that the term applies to all parties, including the reader/listener in his terminology as well. No matter what the language, the difference between "their language" and "his language" proves to be absolutely no obstacle to interaction. Miscommunication, in fact, facilitates their memorable, albeit brief, relationship.

While "babariol, babariol, babarian" or their linguistic neighbors are found in almost all manuscripts of the poem, manuscript C replaces the response of the pilgrim to the two ladies with the following: "Tarrababart, marrababelio riben, saramahart." These words, which sound to be a transliterated Arabic, have led to various attempts at translating the passage.[8] E. Lévi-Provençal went as far as to assert that William must have personally known the Arabic language.[9] Because these lines differ from other manuscripts (there are four manuscripts that preserve this poem), István Frank rejected the claims of Arabists, insisting instead that the impudent scribe of manuscript C had changed the words of the poem.[10]

A more recent translation of the stanza places the words in their dialectical Hispano-Arabic context. Patrice Uhl, after showing that manuscript C does not in fact vary from the manuscript tradition, for the other three manuscripts can in fact be genetically linked, making C as valid a source of the "original" as any of the other manuscripts. In addition, the form and metric of C suggest that C was not derived from an earlier manuscript which branched into the four known poems.¹¹ Consequently, the words "Tarrababart, marababelio riben, saramahart" carry the same weight as the "babariol" stanza and lead Uhl to claim their greater authenticity.

Uhl's translation reads, "Tu regardes la porte de l'ignominie, / Femme de Babel, viens! viens! / Il est, avec elle, devenu ardent . . .".¹² Uhl justifies his selection of each word based on his understanding of the Hispano-Arabic dialect. Of particular interest in his reading is the appearance of Babel. This biblical location symbolizing the confusion of language and the inability to communicate fits in well with the problems of intercultural interaction. William's evocation of Babel, even were it only to be understood by the poet himself, reflects the preoccupation with language that accompanied the daily discourse of the pilgrim or knight on crusade.

Yet another event in William's life hints at cross-ethnic interactions. Pope Leo and William V, the troubadour's grandfather, exchanged letters in 1025. Within the letter from Leo is a request that William send to him the "mulam mirabilem," or wonderful mule that he had previously asked for. Leo often used animals as linguistic codes for people, and Jan M. Ziolkowski has suggested that this letter might refer to a particular person.¹³ William V responded:

> As to your request for a mule, I cannot send it to you at present because I do not have one that I would want you to use, and there is none to be found in our land that has horns, or three tails, or five feet, or any other feature that would warrant your calling it wonderful.¹⁴

The wonderful mule would well represent a woman of a different race, due to its combination of difference and uniqueness. William apparently had control over this person, enough to enable him to send it to Leo for his "use." The veiled reference may very well be applied to a foreign slave woman. Once again, the atmosphere surrounding William the troubadour's youth at court points toward exoticism and sexuality through the inclusion of foreign women.

Finally, William IX passed on to Eleanor of Aquitaine an extraordinary rock crystal vase, now found in the Louvre, that he received from the Muslim king of Zaragoza in the early twelfth century. This vase shows an amicable relationship between William and a Muslim ruler, adding yet another dimension to the already convincing argument that William was quite familiar with the Muslim world and its cultural riches.¹⁵

William's poetry reflects the concerns of his multi-cultural world. The presence of Saracen slave women in his father's court (and mostly likely in his own court) and the encounters with Muslims and Arabs on crusade were just some of the many situations when medieval man could encounter different ethnic and linguistic groups. The obsession with interaction would have been very real to William's contemporaries who had dealings on military, economic, and social levels with the Saracen Other. William's poetry indicates an optimism in the outcome of such interaction. Both difference and similarity are depicted in his poems. Physical discrepancies, like the various languages, are not denied, but are almost prized. These differences create uniqueness and even facilitate interaction. The most base and basic instincts are shared between different peoples, so that superficial characteristics such as race and language can and will be overcome.

William's interracial poetic dealings, however, are basically anti-social. The coding required for the she-mule glosses a relationship that cannot be openly discussed, a relationship that would be condemned by society on several levels. Societal fear of miscegenation demands an envelope of secrecy. Likewise, the two women also need silence from their intercourse with the pilgrim. The pilgrim is taken to be a foreigner, so the fear of interracial intercourse could be the root of their pact of silence, but their status as women is equally likely to require discretion on the part of their love-slave. As later law codes will show, the penalties for women having sex with foreigners were much harsher than those imposed upon men, requiring death in certain situations. Hiding their affair is not simply a matter of good taste but quite possibly of life and death.

Neither text indicates the same woman-on-a-pedestal attitude taken toward women of the same culture as the poet, either. Foreign women are sexualized objects whose only role is to fulfill the needs of either the passer-through or the slave-owner. Convincing arguments have been made that the woman-on-a-pedestal theme is equally misogynistic, but the fact remains that the foreign and local woman are treated differently. While the medieval wife and the slave woman may have shared the brunt of male-centered social aggression, the status of the two was dissimilar. One could live openly in her sphere of society while the other was treated as a mixed source of pleasure and shame.

Writing a generation later than William of Aquitaine was another inveterate traveler, Cercamon (c. 1135), whose name literally means "circle-the-globe." Cercamon's poetry portrays a world where difference and distance are once again the focus of his attention. The opening stanzas of *Ab lo temps qe.s fai refreschar* set the scene for the poet's crisis of communication:

> lo segle e.[ls pratz] reverdezir,
> vueil un novel chant comenzar
> d'un'amor cui am e dezir;
> mas tant s'es de mi loignada
> q'ieu non la puesc acoseguir,
> ni de mos digz no s'agrada.[16]

> [With the season which renews the world, and makes the meadows green again, I wish to begin a new song about a love which I love and desire; but she is so distant from me that I cannot reach her, nor does she take pleasure in my words.[17]]

The opening line evokes the shared world of the lover and the beloved. The coming of spring is a universal element that draws the thoughts of the poet toward his distant love. The sense of what is shared is quickly overshadowed by the gulf of difference that separates and precludes their love. The poet laments the spatial separation of the lovers, and with his words "non la puesc acoseguir," he hints not only that he cannot be in her presence now, but that quite possibly he will never be able to reach her. The hopelessness of their relationship is sealed with his words, "de mos digz no s'agrada." From the perspective of the poet, the fact that she does not take pleasure in his words intensifies his despair. His words of love are what make him unique and desirable among men. If he cannot share this very essence of himself, how is the woman ever to love him? In a world where poems were quite often sent with minstrels or even written down and performed throughout courtly society, the inability of the poet's words to reach his lover could very well indicate a deeper and more serious problem. The only permanent block to the woman's hearing of his love, in his words, would be if the two did not share the same language. The poetic word resists translation, and the poet loses his power to please the object of his affection.

For Cercamon, the foreign woman is no longer fetishized as sexual object. She shares the same shaky pedestal as her Western counterpart. The obstacles of love that inspire troubadour poetry, such as the jealous husband, the court slanderers, and protective entourage do not appear in this poem. His deterrents take on monolithic proportions. The barrier which separates the two is practically insurmountable, and even if it were not, the problem of verbal intercourse would remain irresolvable. This new perspective on long-distance and intercultural love assumes social similarity, unlike William's poems. The woman deserves veneration and courtly poetry, and the reader/listener is led to believe that if she could understand his words she would love him for his poetic prowess. Nonetheless, the poem focuses on difference, rather than sameness. The foreign woman presents an obstacle to the lover the likes of which the common troubadour has never encountered. Cercamon challenges his contemporaries to find a more difficult situation than his own, and the implication is that such a scenario could not exist. For the poet/lover, the foreign woman thus assumes the quality of the ultimate dare; Cercamon has created the most impossible love-situation, therefore he triumphs as poet over his fellow troubadours. Cercamon turns William's situation on its head, showing that lack of communication cannot facilitate real love.

Jaufré Rudel (1130–1170) echoes Cercamon, again illustrating the troubadours' concern with problems of communication. *Qan lo rius de la fontana* takes the theme of distant love and resultant lack of intercourse as its central concern. His explicit comparison in the third stanza of his love with Christian, Jewish, and Saracen women makes this poem particularly pertinent to discussions of interreligious or interracial love. The second two stanzas read:

Amors de terra loindana,
per vos totz lo cors mi do;
e non puosc trobar meizina
si non vau al sieu reclam
ab atraich d'amor doussana,
dinz vergier o sotz cortina
ab desirada compaigna.

Pois del tot m'en faill aizina,
no.m meravill s'ieu m'aflam,
car anc genser Crestiana
non fo, que Dieus non la vol,
Juzeva ni Sarrazina;
et es ben paisutz de manna
qui ren de s'amor gazaigna.

[Love from a distant land, / For you my whole self aches; / and I can find no remedy / Unless I go at her call / With the lure of sweet love, In a garden or beneath a curtain / With a desired companion.
Since I get no relief at all, / I am not surprised if I am aflame, / For there was never a nobler Christian woman, / A Jewess or a Saracen, / For God does not wish that there be ; / And whoever gains any of her love / Is well fed with manna.[18]]

The "amors de terra loindana" may well already be a banal theme at the time Jaufré composes these verses. The only remedy he can find for his obsession is physical proximity, evidently impossible since "del tot m'en faill aizina." Jaufré must prove his love truly unique, however, and worthy of his devotion. He exalts her by stating that "anc genser Crestiana no fo...Juzeva ni Sarrazina." In this statement, Jaufré implies that other poets may have sung of all of these women, Christian, Jew, and Saracen. He finds all of these women meriting poetic praise, though not to the same degree as his special love. By not naming the religion of his beloved, Jaufré in fact fabricates a poem that could be used for all women that Western men encounter. His poem creates the universal subject, and when he sends the song to Lord Hugh [tramet lo vers que chantam plan et en lenga romana a.N Hugon Brun[19]] he gives a poetic gift that could in turn be bestowed upon any woman of his choosing. His use of "lenga romana," or Romance, implies as well a universalism, as the language of the troubadours was a *koiné* in courts throughout the West.

Jaufré's *Qan lo rius de la fontana* has a varied manuscript tradition, with some elements of the poem changing dramatically from text to text while other elements remain constant. Sarah Kay, in exploring the continuations of the text, reads the differences as textual criticism by thirteenth-century authors. She concludes:

> The manuscript tradition of Rudel's songs reveals that a number of not very talented versifiers from about the thirteenth century saw him as a moralist or a conventional love poet.[20]

Kay contrasts this older reading with modern criticism centering upon the mystical and crusading interpretations of recent criticism. The final stanza where Jaufré sends his poem to "N. Peire Ug" does not repeat itself in versions outside the U manuscript. Not privileging the criticism of the continuations, Kay in facts opines that perhaps the unique character of this crusading stanza lends credence to its genuine nature. She questions, rightfully so, whether Jaufré could have "authorized" all versions of the poem, as Rupert Pickens contends in his edition of Jaufré Rudel's corpus, so one version may very well be closer to Jaufré's original poem.

While *Qan lo rius de la fontana* enables communication between a lover and a ubiquitous beloved, one of Jaufré's poems has come to represent the entire poetic corpus of love at a distance and the dilemma of intercourse. Perhaps one of the most commented-upon poems in medieval literature, Jaufré Rudel's 52-line poem "Lanqan li jorn son lonc en mai" continues to elude classification. The poem refers to two people: Jaufré's *amor de lonh* and the *pairís* who condemns the poet to love without being loved in return. Critics tend to align themselves into camps: those who think that these persons can be historically identified and those who believe they cannot. The *vida* of Jaufré Rudel, written some 100 years after the poet's death, qualifies as the first recorded instance of historical interpretation. According to the *vida*, Jaufré's *amor de lonh* is the *comtessa de Tripol*. In the late nineteenth century, Gaston Paris entered the fray, positing that the *vida* was constructed from the poetry itself. Thus, interpreting the poem based on the vida would result in circular reasoning. In 1942, Grace Frank warned the academic community:

> If then we do not assume a real love-affair for every modern love-lyric, how incredibly naive it is to attempt after the lapse of some eight hundred years, and with only pseudo-historical romances to guide us, to identify the ladies of the troubadours.[21]

She proceeded to hypothesize that the *amor de lonh* was in fact an allegorical mistress, referring to the pilgrim/crusader Jaufré's desire to visit the Holy Land. Ironically, Frank thus enters into the camp of the historically-oriented, for while she does not identify a particular person as Jaufré's mistress, she reads the poem as a reflection of Jaufré's personal history.

Leo Spitzer takes up Frank's thesis with a structural reading of the poem. Spitzer sees no need to look outside the poem for a woman. For him, the goal of the poet is to explore the nature of love through paradox: being and seeming, possessing and not possessing, or in Spitzer's words:

> l'entre-deux psychologique dans lequel se place le sentiment de l'amour, senti comme réel et pourtant irréel, passant du dreit nien jusqu'a l'occupation de tout notre être.[22]

Not surprisingly, one recent article has gone with the anti-structuralist, New Historicist approach. While the *vida* is taken to be unreliable in and of itself, other historical sources are mined to produce a reading. Not only is the mysterious *amor de lonh* identified, but the poem previously seen by Spitzer as a pure embodiment of the love sentiment is fashioned into a political tool: a crusading song designed to recruit fighters.[23]

Jaufré's poem has suffered over the last century from an outpouring of divisive criticism. However, a certain *rapprochement* of the two camps can be accomplished. While the poem cannot be divorced from its moment of historical creation, it **can**, nevertheless, still function as an expression of love without historical external referent when read as an articulation of mystical love. The *vida* glosses this love a century later, following the Albigensian Crusade, to make what was mystical in conception become concrete, historical and, most importantly, acceptable to the Church.

The middle of the twelfth century saw an explosion of heretical sects in the south of France, where Jaufré Rudel was composing his verses. Little is known of the origin of the various belief systems, but Jaufré's poem reveals a mystical orientation which the Andalusian Muslim Ibn al-'Arabî (1165–1240) would later describe as follows:

> Love never becomes connected to anything but the nonexistent thing—that which has no existence when the connection becomes established. Love desires the existence or occurrence of its object. . . . What the lover loves is the desire of union with the specific person, whoever it might be. If it is someone who can be embraced, he loves embracing his beloved. . . . Hence his love only becomes attached to that of the person which is nonexistent at the moment, but he imagines that he loves that person.[24]

Jaufré's "Lanqan li jorn" reveals that same desire for union with his faraway beloved. In stanza I, he tells of the faraway love which cannot be cured by the coming of the spring. The songs of the "auzèlhs de lonh" which come to the speaking subject (who from now on will be referred to as "the poet") are a painful reminder of the absence of love. Indeed, this month of love, May, can only bring sorrow, and it is no better to him than "l'iverns gelatz."

The next three stanzas compose the poet's fantasy of his reunion with his beloved. The second stanza outlines the journey he will undergo to reach her. The repetition of *lonh* twice in each stanza reiterates the beloved's absence. In the third stanza, he imagines the moment he will be near her, "Près de lièis, si be'm sui de lonh/Adonc parrà'l parlamens fins",[25] when they will share the conversation of lovers. The separation of the lovers is the subject of the fourth stanza. Doubt that he will ever reach her also creeps in at this point. The fifth and sixth stanzas treat the intense desire he has to undertake this voyage to meet the beloved. But the seventh stanza introduces the real ambiguity of the poem, the point that relates the poet's desire to the kind of mysticism outlined by Ibn al-'Arabî. The poet laments:

> Ver ditz qui m'apèla lechai
> Ni desiron d'amor de lonh,
> Car nulhs autres jòis tan no'm plai
> Com jauzimens d'amor de lonh.[26]
> [He speaks the truth who calls me covetous / And desirous of love from afar / For no other joy pleases me so much / as enjoyment of love from afar.[27]]

The last two lines are particularly significant, for he claims that no other joy is as pleasing as his "amor de lonh." The ambiguity of this assertion allows the interpretation that it is not the beloved he loves as much as the desire for the beloved. The *pairìs* who has cast a spell which curses the love not to be returned has not in fact created an obstacle to the lover, for the obstacle to union is more important to this love than the beloved herself. The final doubling of obstacles, the curse as well as the excessive distance separating the lovers, attests to the central role of the obstacle in this relationship. Love, as Ibn al-'Arabî would attest, can endure only as long as it remains unfulfilled. The *vida* corroborates this reading, portraying Jaufré as expiring in the arms of his beloved when he finally reaches her.

The poet casts himself as of a pilgrim in the second stanza, a role which has frequently led to an allegorical interpretation of the poem. When he says, "Ai! qar me fos lai pelegrís,/Si que mos fustz e mos tapís/Fos pels sieus bèlhs uèlhs remiratz!"[28] [Ah, would that I were a pilgrim there / So that my staff and cloak might be reflected in her beautiful eyes],[29] the poet places the beloved in the position of a sacred pilgrimage site. The beloved could, in fact, be equated with God; her gaze upon the pilgrim is the final destination of the traveler. The conflation of the beloved with God is a familiar concept in medieval Islamic mysticism, where the writings of Ibn al-'Arabî are again useful:

> Though no one loves any but his own Creator, he is veiled from Him by the love for Zaynab, Su'âd, Hind, Laylâ, this world, money, position, and everything loved in the world. Poets exhaust their words writing about all these existent things without knowing, but the Gnostics never hear a verse, a riddle, a panegyric, or a love poem that is not about Him, hidden beyond the veils of forms.[30]

Jaufré's poetry can be read in this vein; not as an allegory or as blasphemy, but as a celebration that all human love is also love for God. The desire that the poet shows for his human *amor de lonh* is real, not allegorical, but it cannot be separated from his desire for union with God.

The Arabic poetic tradition of Jaufré's period used mystical and multiple referents in much of its love lyric corpus. The great mystic and philosopher, Ibn al-'Arabî, wrote love lyric as well, often more sensual and physical than that of the troubadours. But he also wrote commentaries on his own poetry, explaining each desire as a desire for union with God, each love as a longing for the creator. These commentaries parallel the *vida* written for Jaufré Rudel, except that the two glosses act in opposite ways. While Ibn al-'Arabî embraces his mysticism, the *vida*, written long after Jaufré's death, serves to anthropomorphize the love of the poet. The *amor de lonh* is turned into an historical personage, the Countess of Tripoli. Jaufré's journey to see her and subsequent death in her arms is fairly clearly drawn from the poetry itself, and "Lanquan li jorn" in specific provides most of the fodder for the author of the *vida*. Between the time Jaufré wrote (c. 1150) and the date of the *vida* (c. 1250), the forces of Simon de Monfort and Louis VIII had devastated the south of France in crusades leveled against those the Pope had named heretics. During that time, someone had lovingly collected the poetry of the troubadours into manuscripts and added a *vida* to each of their works. In the case of Jaufré, the *vida* they wrote ensured that the poetry would continue to be read. The *vida* dissociates the poetry from the mystical movements that had been only recently eradicated. The tension between the mysticism of the poetry and its unlikely historicization, a strain reflected in current criticism, is thus not relieved by denying the role of history, but by realizing that the poetry and the *vida*, while embedded in the historical circumstances of the period, need not, in fact, be histories themselves.

No *sap chantar qui so non di* talks of the inability to interact with a love whom he has never met, nor will he ever—a theme that many of his poems address. In his examination of what he terms the cycle of "l'*amors de Terra Lonhdana*," Yves Lefèvre has also found the poetry of Jaufré Rudel to express mystical sentiment. He, however, interprets the *amors de terra lonhdana* to be literally a love for the distant land itself. Since Jaufré's link to the Crusades and crusaders suggests a personal involvement with the Holy Land, Lefèvre reads Jaufré's poem as a pre-departure manifesto, explaining his love for and longing to travel to Jerusalem. Thus for Lefèvre, communication is blocked between Jaufré and his beloved because the beloved is inanimate:

> La Terre Sainte, qui n'est pas une femme, ne jouira jamais de la présence de Jaufré; elle ne pourra pas lui manifester les sentiments qu'aurait une femme, le choisir comme ami, faire avec lui un pacte amoureux.[31]

While Lefèvre's lack of insistence on a historical personage is refreshing, he replaces one physical, singular referent (a woman beloved) with another (a distant land). The inability or refusal to respond to the words of love need not indicate actual muteness or even distance, but rather a block at the level of social interaction. The non-responsive beloved, a staple of mystical love lyric, need not refer to a single object but rather to a multiplicity of referents.

The opening phrase of the poem, from which it draws its modern title, "*No sap chantar qui so non di*," sets the theme of the poem within the problems of expression. How can a poet make love to a woman with whom he cannot speak or whom he cannot see? The Holy Land indeed fits the criteria of the poem— Jaufré can neither see nor speak to it, assuming that he has composed the poem while in the West. This reading, however, trivializes the problem of language to express the desire of the poet. This dilemma is omnipresent for the troubadours of this period, but within the context of the period, the possibility of multiple languages and foreign lovers cannot be excluded. The poem can refer to all of these referents at once, multiplicity being the key to reading mystical, multi-leveled poetry. The far-away land, the foreign woman, even the local, inaccessible woman can all be implied within the same verses. The poem takes on a multitude of meanings, depending on the occasion and the intentions of the poet, the singer, and the audience. Jaufré's poetic history is contingency.

Troubadour poetry, while not history, contains within its lines the experience of a particular historical moment. The poetry, not intending to function as a cultural gloss, nonetheless cannot escape the environment of its composition. Menocal believes that in reading troubadour poetry:

> ... perhaps paradoxically, I would argue that the best reading we can do of this poetry, that which does least violence to the hermeneutic distance it wishes to create with all readers except the True Believers (who scarcely need our critical comments), is one that reunites it with its peculiar and highly complex historical circumstances. Sometimes, memory is contingency.[32]

A noble goal, but how can the modern reader unite the historical and the mystical of another place and time?

Language in these texts provides only one of many ways of approaching the medieval text. The problems of language and communication are omnipresent, and the modern reader can historicize the struggle of the medieval poet while remaining within the realm of what is known and knowable to the modern reader. In particular, the experience of post-colonial writers and their audiences makes an intriguing parallel with the question of language in medieval poetry. Post-colonial critics have elaborated the role of language in cross-cultural communication, and in modifying their theories, we can better read the mystical thirteenth-century text. As Ngugi Wa Thiong'o, the Kenyan author and critic, has written, the link between language and culture is inseparable:

> Values are the basis of a people's identity, their sense of particularity as members of the human race. All this is carried by language. Language as culture is the collective memory bank of a people's experience in history. Culture is almost indistinguishable from the language that makes possible its genesis, growth, banking, articulation, and indeed its transmission from one generation to the next. . . .[33]

Thus the troubadour crisis in communication with the beloved reveals an inability for the communication of culture between two peoples. If communication is the basis of evolving culture, then the lack of communication indicates the stagnation of culture itself.

In the post-colonial text, the problems of communication lie between authors and their readers. The author may write in one language, say English, but the audience of the author may well not understand English or have it as a second language rather than a mother tongue. Authors finds themselves writing in second languages as well. Writing in the author's mother tongue is not always practical, for the number of speakers of that language may be quite small and thus the audience reduced in numbers. English universalizes the message but also renders it opaque or invisible for certain desired readers.

The love poetry of the troubadours involves three persons, real or fictive, in its linguistic event: the author (poet), the reader/listener, and the beloved. Communication in these texts is not restricted to the author-reader relationship in the post-colonial novel. The block in understanding operates simultaneously at the levels of author-reader/listener and author-beloved. What may be clearly decoded at one level can be opaque at another level. When William's pilgrim responds with his cryptic "Babariol, babariol, Babarian," the women of the text decode one meaning in his message ("I do not speak your language") and respond appropriately. The reader/listener, however, while understanding the poem to that point, cannot make meaning from that phrase and multiple readings of that phrase result. The poet enables communication on one level in severing it on another.

Lack of communication, a topos as has been shown in troubadour poetry, is the site of cultural difference. If cultural interaction is equivalent with communication, then as Bill Ashcroft writes of understanding:

> The central feature of such activity is presence, the presence of the speaker and the hearer to each other constituting language as communication.[34]

For the post-colonial writer, a huge distance, both physical and cultural, prevents total communication between author and reader. Indeed no text is completely transparent, offering complete understanding of the author's intent to any reader. However, reading across cultural boundaries amplifies the distance between the reader and the author. The resultant lack of understanding marks the moment of difference. In the post-colonial text, this silence, or absence of communication, has been termed the "metonymic gap."[35] The metonymic gap enables meaning rather than destroying it, but that meaning is multiple and includes a distinct awareness of cultural difference between the author and the reader. The two parties involved in the message event know that when moments of opaqueness occur within the reading of the cross-cultural text, an extra meaning or meanings denoting cultural difference arise.

The distant love of Jaufré and Cercamon embodies the conflict and resolution of the cross-cultural text. The gulf of silence between the lover and the beloved, and indeed the physical distance between the two of them, does not obliterate meaning but rather creates the opportunity for a different type of meaning. Within the metonymic gap between poet and beloved, the reader/listener marks the moment of difference. The reader/listener identifies with the poet, who cannot communicate with the beloved. Lack of communication signals cultural disparity. When the poet succeeds in making himself understood to the beloved, as in William's song, the reader/listener experiences at that moment the ambiguous and unsettling sense of difference with both the poet and his beloved (which explains, perhaps, the intense critical interest in those moments of utter opaqueness on the part of the reader/listener). The poet can thus shift his alliances, either being "like" the reader or "like" the beloved, but unable to achieve transparency with both parties.

As the modern reader approaches the medieval mystical text, reading within the cultural history of the period, as Menocal suggests, requires a not-so-difficult identification with the problems of miscommunication. Once the reader crosses the original metonymic gap, that is, mastering the language of the poet, within the text are additional lapses of understanding. Just as the modern reader can never achieve full transparency with an Old Provençal text (or, as has been argued, with any text, though the level of opaqueness is undoubtedly higher with a long unused language), the mystical text prohibits full understanding through insertion of intentional items of cultural opaqueness. The troubadours, by focusing on the impasse of intercourse between lover and beloved, celebrate the opportunities that this lack of full understanding can provide. The text exists because of and through the understanding that it fails to create, spawning other meanings and alternative interpretations for both the modern and the thirteenth-century listener/reader. Needless to say, these moments may not and perhaps should not be the same for the modern and the contemporary audiences, yet the process remains constant and the text creates its interest and meaning through this process.

William IX, Cercamon and Jaufré Rudel experienced contact with Arab culture in very different ways. Yet each faced the same problem of communicating new relationships that could not be contained in the epic model. These new songs had to be sung in order to show that Christians and Saracens could be much more than enemies on the battlefield. Dijkstra and Gosman demonstrate that for the crusade lyric, three different factors come into play to define the genre: outside historical reality, deformation of that reality, and the intersection of the distorted (fictive) view of reality with the poetic world.[36] In the case of the three poets studied here, they likely experienced real, historical interaction with Muslim women. Their own interpretations of these interactions resulted in a personal, not necessarily distorted, view of reality. As they sought creative outlet to describe relationships that did not previously exist, they turned to the lyric with its tensions of communication and deferred desire: a totally appropriate venue for a difficult, new situation. Indeed, lyric captured a specific moment in Christian-Muslim history, a moment that would soon give way to other historical pressures and consequent genres.

NOTES

1. The question of Arabic influence on Provencal poetry has a long, virulent history. The essentials of the argument can be found in the first chapter of María Menocal's, *The Arabic Role in Medieval Literary History: A Forgotten Heritage* (Philadelphia: University of Pennsylvania Press, 1979).
2. Charles Melville and Ahmad Ubaydli, *Christians and Moors in Spain: Volume III Arabic Sources* (711–1501) (Warminster, England: Aris & Phillips, 1992), p. 71.
3. Reinhart Pieter Anne Dozy, *Recherches sur l'histoire et la littérature de l'Espagne pendant le moyen age* (Leyde: E. J. Brill, 1881), p. 341. Vincent de Bartholomaeis echoes this story in his Old French translation of Amatus of Montecassino , in "Storia de' Normanni di Amato di Montecassino volgarizzata in antico francese," *Fonti per la storia d'Italia, pubblicata dall' Istituto storico italiano per il Medio Evo Scrittori*. Secolo XI (Rome: Tipografia del Senato, 1935), pp. 14–15.
4. Menocal, op. cit., p. 32.
5. *Les Chansons de Guillaume IX, duc d'Aquitaine*, ed. A. Jeanroy (Paris: Champion, 1927), V, lines 19–30.
6. Jeanroy, op. cit., translates "latin" as language.
7. Michel Stanesco's reading of the poem concurs with the belief that the imagery is sexual, linking the blood, sex and symbolic death of the pilgrim to a coming-of-age ritual. His reading contradicts earlier feeling that the poem reflects childishness and poor taste on the part of the troubadour, lending more credence to readings of the poem, such as this one. See Michel Stanesco, "L'étrange aventure d'un faux muet : blessures symboliques et performances sexuelles dans un poème de Guillaume IX d'Aquitaine," *Cahiers de Civilisation Médiévale* 32 (2) (1989), pp. 115–124.
8. See A. R. Nykl, *Troubadour Studies. A Critical Survey of Recent Books Published in This Field*, Cambridge, MA (1944), p. 4, n. 9.
9. E. Lévi-Provençal, "Poésie arabe d'Espagne et poésie d'Europe médiévale," *Islam d'Occident. Études d'histoire médiévale* (Paris: G.P. Maisonneuve, 1948), p. 299.
10. Istv·n Frank, "Babariol babarian dans Guillaume IX," *Romania* 73 (1952), pp. 227–234.
11. Patrice Uhl, "Farai un vers, pos mi sonelh : la version du chansonnier C (B.N., Fr. 856), la cobla bilingue et le problème du lati ou Tarrababart saramahart dans Guillaume IX d'Aquitaine," *Cahiers de Civilisation Médiévale* 33 (1) (1990), pp. 29–30.
12. Ibid., p. 37.
13. Jan M. Ziolkowski, *Talking Animals: medieval Latin beast poetry, 750–1150* (Philadelphia: University of Pennsylvania Press, 1993), p. 121.
14. Ibid., p. 121.
15. George T. Beech, "Troubadour Contacts with Muslim Spain and Knowledge of Arabic: New Evidence Concerning William IX of Aquitaine," *Romania* 113 (1992–95), p. 34.
16. Wolf and Rosenstein, *The Poetry of Cercamon and Jaufré Rudel* (New York: Garland, 1983), p. 45, lines 1–7.
17. Ibid., p. 45.
18. Ibid., pp. 138–39.

19. Ibid., p. 140, lines 30–31.
20. Sarah Kay, "Continuation as Criticism: The Case of Jaufre Rudel," *Medium Aevum* 56(1) (1987), p. 56.
21. Grace Frank, "The Distant Love of Jaufré Rudel," *Modern Language Notes* 57 (1942), p. 534.
22. Leo Spitzer, "L'Amour lointain de Jaufré Rudel," *Romanische Literaturstudien* (Tübingen: M. Niemeyer, 1959), p. 390.
23. Roy Rosenstein, "New Perspectives on Distant Love: Jaufré Rudel, Uc Bru, and Sarrazina," *Modern Philology* 87 (3) (1990), p. 235.
24. William Chittick, *The Sufi Path of Knowledge* (Albany: SUNY Press, 1989), p. 389.
25. Wolf, op. cit., lines 18–19.
26. Ibid., lines 43–46.
27. *The Songs of Jaufré Rudel*. ed. Rupert Pickens (Toronto: University of Toronto Press, 1977), p. 169.
28. Wolf, op. cit., lines 12–14.
29. *The Songs of Jaufré Rudel*, op. cit., p. 167.
30. Chittick, op. cit., p. 181.
31. Yves Lefèvre, "L'Amors de Terra Lonhdana dans les chansons de Jaufré Rudel," in *Mélanges offerts Rita Lejeune* (Gembloux: Duculot, 1968), p. 194.
32. María Rosa Menocal, *Shards of Love* (Durham,NC: Duke University Press, 1994), pp. 86–87.
33. Bill Ashcroft, "Constitutive Graphonomy," in *The Post-Colonial Studies Reader* (New York: Routledge, 1995), p. 289.
34. Ibid., p. 298.
35. Ibid., p. 299.
36. Cathrynke Dijkstra and Martin Gosman, "Poetic Fiction and Poetic Reality: the Case of the Romance Crusade Lyrics," *Neophilologus* 79 (1995), p. 22.

4. New Songs with New Rhythms: The Romance Epic

> They rediscovered the old songs—they had never completely lost touch with them—and reshaped them to meet the new needs of their struggle. They also created new songs and dances with new rhythms where the old ones were found inadequate.[1]

Exterminans. The tenth-century *Beatus de Morgan* so names the enemy of the faithful, the two-faced monsters that the Christian soldier combats in a miniature that decorates the page. This enemy, the Infidel, has a hideous, terrifying countenance, but it also has a seductive, beautiful, *feminine* side:

> ...une sorte de couronne à reflets dorés leur casquait la tête; leur face était presque humaine, leur chevelure ressemblait à celle des femmes, leurs dents à celles de lions. . . .[2]

This dual nature of the Infidel is central to the medieval perspective of the Muslim. The enemy is at once an exotic beast and a lovely woman. It attracts as it kills. The Infidel is both things at once, but never entirely one or the other. *Chansons de geste* of the twelfth and thirteenth centuries depict this split view of the Saracen. Rising from the songs of desire of the troubadours and the conflicted image of the Saracen warrior, the epic Saracen can be black or white, lovely or hideous, helpful or treacherous—or any combination of these. The newest element of the French imaginings of the Saracen is the appearance of the female Saracen. Whereas she was voiceless and abstract in troubadour song and virtually absent in the earliest male-centered epics, now the female Saracen takes center stage. The ambiguous, always ambivalent but now feminine, view of the Muslim and its historical context is the subject of this chapter.

Together with a change in the relationship between Christian and Muslim, the twelfth century saw the explosion of a new genre, the *chanson de geste*. The *chansons de geste* serve as an appropriate lesson in the history and culture of the period. While the stories that the *chansons* told made no outright claims to veracity, the line between history and fiction was often intentionally blurred. As Gabrielle Spiegel noted in referring to prose historiography:

> Especially in the Middle Ages, historical writing, precisely to the degree that it claimed to be free of imaginative elaboration, served as a vehicle of ideological elaboration.[3]

The *chansons de geste* did not make the same outright pretension of truth that thirteenth-century prose historiography would, but nonetheless there was a strange intermingling of fact and fiction in these tales. Some of the motivation for mixing truth and fantasy may have been to serve political or personal ends. For example, the tellers of epics like the *Chanson de Roland* may well have chosen the names of illustrious contemporaries and included them among the entourage of Charlemagne in order to gain patronage for their performances. In addition, certain families commissioned elaborate series of *chansons de geste* in order to establish the "histories" of their families. Though these stories might be largely or even entirely fabricated, they were often presented as factual, and over time their content might even become accepted as an historical account.

While founding family trees and furthering the political ambitions of certain larger houses of power, these tales give models of social interaction as well. The stories give various scenarios of how people of different races, genders, and religions might interact. Without doubt, the models that they present are at times just as highly fabricated as the stories of the exploits of the ancestors of key contemporary political figures. However, the parallel between the establishment of certain families that Spiegel has elaborated and the patterns of social interaction in the *chansons de geste* can be taken further. Just as fanciful stories about family origins shaped the way that listeners perceived those families, so listeners may also have begun to accept as possible the stories of social interaction as presented to them in the *chansons de geste*. For that reason, the factual content of the stories is largely irrelevant to this study. Rather, it is the *perception* of social interaction as created by the stories themselves that becomes uppermost.

As an example that will be discussed further in the context of marriage, the thirteenth-century Spanish law book, *Las Siete Partidas* contains examples and laws that read more like romance than law. The literati of Alfonso X's court no doubt were quite familiar with the omnipresent theme in all genres of literature involving interactions between Saracens and Christians. These stories influenced the author of the *Siete partidas*. By codifying and legitimizing these social roles in a lawbook, the stories took on an historical air in turn. The readers of the *chansons de geste* who might well be sceptical of the reality of the plot line may also have heard that the revered lawbook contained and validated a *chanson de geste*-type tale. At that point, the reader could no longer be quite sure whether the *chansons de geste* they read or heard were true or false. Social relationships are defined by their perception in society; that is, a relationship has a social value only if society deems it to have one. So the imagined interactions put forth by medieval authors must have influenced real relationships in society at large, and when those imagined cases of social interaction became accepted by sectors of society, those images left the realm of the imaginary and moved into officially sanctioned sources like lawbooks. The existence of demonstrable trading relationships and the fact that Christians and Muslims lived side by side in Spain and parts of southern France meant that real relationships gave medieval authors a context in which to develop their imaginary alliances. Thus the fact and fiction of Christian and Muslim social interaction became intermingled and interdependent.

The very earliest stories spoke of Saracens solely in the context of warfare. The *Chanson de Roland* written in the late eleventh or early twelfth century is a prime example. Saracens in this epic are enemies to be conquered and, redoubtable though they may be, their culture does not inspire the imagination of the early poets to the degree it will later authors. In fact, the Saracens are little more than mirror reflections of the French army itself. The *laisses* that describe the gearing up of both armies parallel each other, underlining similarity rather than difference. As Philippe Sénac notes, in the *Chanson de Roland*, Muslim institutions "sont la réplique parfaite de celles de la féodalité."[4]

The other two earliest epics also include Saracens in their cast of characters. The story of Gormont and Isembart, referred to by Hariulf, monk of Saint-Riquier, as early as 1088, comes to the present as a tantalizing fragment which describes the battle between the Saracen leader Gormont, aided by the French turncoat Isembart, and the French King Louis. The epic is most striking for its elegant and admiring description of the Saracen Gormont, who would have been the perfect knight had he not been misled in his religion. Louis, who is mortally wounded in the combat, is in fact the weaker of the two in battle and would surely have lost had God not interceded in the appropriate moment.

In the *Chanson de Guillaume*, Guillaume joins his nephew Vivien to fight the Saracens. Guibourc, Guillaume's Saracen wife, will become a main character in the *Prise d'Orange*, but for the moment, she is simply mentioned in passing. Like the *Chanson de Roland* and *Gormont et Isembart*, the geste focuses on the fighting relationships between the men involved in the story. Once again, the prowess of the Saracens is admired, and in the *Guillaume* the possibility of cooperation makes an appearance in the Saracen companions of Vivien, Girard and Guischard. In a relationship which inverts that of Gormont and Isembart, the Saracens reject their people to cast their lots with the French. However, Guibourc and her brother, the Saracen giant Rainouart, steal the show from all the other characters in later stories that were added to the cycle.

These three epics, the *Chanson de Roland*, the *Chanson de Guillaume*, and *Gormont et Isembart*, are generally taken to be the earliest *chansons de geste* and the only ones given a definitive date preceding 1150. Their aim is different and their vision of the world is much more limited than succeeding songs. To lump all *chansons de geste* together, as Sénac does, gives an ahistorical notion of genre uncalled for when reading these texts. After 1150 there is a veritable explosion of texts which treat the Saracen and Christian relationship in a different context. While the comic exploits of Rainouart captured the attention of the medieval reader in one series of texts, the literary "sisters" of Guibourc, Saracen women who interact with Christian men, must be counted as the most popular figures in the corpus of *chansons de geste* that dominate literary activity in the twelfth and thirteenth centuries.

The development of multifaceted depictions of Saracens coincided with the great translation push of the twelfth and thirteenth centuries. Peter the Venerable engaged several translators, including one Muslim, during the course of his visit to Spain in the 1140s. Marie-Thérèse d'Alverny characterizes this period of interest in things Arabic as the result of the beginnings of the *Reconquista*:

> Sur les pas des armées d'Alphonse, des étudiants, venus de tous pays, accouraient en Espagne pour découvrir les trésors de la science au fond des "armaria" des infidèles dont le prestige intellectuel semblait croître à mesure que s'effaçait leur domination politique.[5]

The new *chansons de geste*, albeit representing a fantastic view of the Saracen, seem to be inspired by this rush for knowledge. While the audience of the *chansons de geste* might not have been interested in the translations of Galen and the Koran effected by men like Peter and Mark of Toledo, they too longed to know more about Saracen culture. Inverted French models were no longer enough to satisfy the *chansons de geste* audience, and stories were told which included new characters (for example, Rainouart and the Saracen princess) and new situations. Just as Peter the Venerable was mindful to remark in a letter to Saint Bernard that his translation of the Koran was commissioned in order to better know and defeat the heresy of Islam,[6] so the stories of the epic Saracen were careful to mention the ever-present problem of non-Christian beliefs. But aside from that one problem, the Saracen could be anything his or her Christian counterpart was and, quite often, even more.

C. Meredith Jones was prompted to remark in 1942 that the portrait of the epic Saracen is:

> ... utterly useless as a guide to students of mediaeval manners and customs. It is based on hate, on a deliberately false propaganda. Its object was to disfigure, and the few instances in which there is a more or less faithful representation of reality are accidental.[7]

Indeed the vision of the Saracen could be grotesque and vulgar at times. In *Aliscans* (second half of the twelfth century) Guillaume explains to Esmeré, son of his wife Guibourc by a previous marriage, why he is attacking the

Saracens:

> Puis que li hom n'aime crestïenté,
> Et qu'il het Deu et despit charité,
> N'a droit en vie, jel di par verité,
> Et qui l'ocist, si destruit un maufé[8]

> [Since the man does not love Christianity and he hates God and despises goodness, it is not proper that he should live. I am telling the truth. He who kills him thus destroys an evil-doer]

The poet of *Aliscans* has earlier described the Saracen:

> Cest une gens dou plus divers samblant,
> Tot sont cornu derire et devant[9]

> [They are a people of the most aberrant appearance. All are horned back and front.]

However, it must be remembered that Guillaume's much-loved wife is also of Saracen origin. Just as the poet and Guillaume speak ill of "Saracens" in general, they also clearly exclude some Saracens from their condemnation. Jones' remarks fail to show that portrayal of the epic Saracen was not limited to these images designed to provoke disgust. As with Gormont, even the warrior could be described in terms of admiration. The Saracen princess, who has been the object of quite a few probing articles,[10] shows well the ambiguity that the Christian author experienced in depicting Muslims. While Jones finds the often-magical abilities of the epic female to be yet another example of distortion and denigration,[11] her extraordinary powers can better be interpreted as positive qualities. She has an aptitude to act, charm, seduce, and succeed that her Christian counterpart simply does not possess.[12]

The theme of the Saracen princess who aids a captured French knight and later marries him is found in seventeen different chansons de geste. Her popularity is well described by Joseph Bédier, who wrote:

> ... mais dans combien de poèmes ne la voyons-nous pas reparaître, toujours la même, plus blanche que neige en février ou que fleur d'épine...elle possède donc un ensemble de qualités parfaites, et n'a qu'un défaut, *Quant Dieu ne croit, le fils sainte Marie*.[13]

A major theme of the twelfth century, the origins of the theme of the Saracen princess were located by F. M. Warren in a rhetorical exercise posed by Seneca for use in the classroom. His sixth *controversia* reads:

> Captus a piratis scripsit patri de redemptione. Non redimebatur. Arcipiratae filia jurare eum coegit, ut duceret se uxorem si dimissus esset. Relicto patre secuta est adulescentem. Rediit ad patrem, duxit illam. Orba

incidit. Pater imperat ut arcipiratae filiam dimittat et orbem ducat. Nolentem abdicat.[14]

[A man captured by pirates wrote to his father about a ransom. He was not ransomed. The daughter of the pirate chief forced him to swear to marry her if he was let go. He swore. She left her father and followed the young man. He returned to his father and married the girl. An orphan appeared on the scene; the father orders his son to divorce the daughter of the pirate chief and marry the orphan. He refuses. His father disinherits him.[15]]

Students are to argue whether or not the young man should keep his promise. In Seneca's version, religion is not the main stumbling block in the relation between the two young people, but rather race or social status. The daughter of a pirate (even the "arcipirata"!) is presumably not an appropriate marriage partner for a young man of a stable family, a family who could have been expected to redeem their captured son.

The daughter of the archenemy who aids a prisoner to escape makes its appearance in Europe around 1135 with the story of Bohemond and Melaz found in Orderic Vitalis's *Historia Ecclesiastica*. This story is particularly remarkable in that it is found in an historical text, and is a story that Orderic Vitalis clearly wrote believing it to have taken place. Melaz is a strong and much-admired woman even before meeting the Christian crusaders:

> Melaz filia Dalimanni principis pulchra erat et multum sapiens, et in omni domo patris sui magnam potestatem habens . . .

> [Melaz, the daughter of the Danishmend, was beautiful and very wise; she had much authority in her father's house.[16]]

Having spent much time talking with the Christians as they languish in her father's prison, Melaz decides to free Bohemond and his followers. Their words sway her to accept Christianity, and she makes them promise that she will be married to Bohemond. Upon her release, however, Bohemond points out that he will make a most unsuitable husband as he has many more wars to fight and will be absent a great deal. He makes a deal with her, offering his cousin:

> Ecce Rogerius Ricardi principis soboles consobrinus meus est me iunior aetate, excellens uenustate, par nobilitate, diuitiis et potestate.

> [See now Roger, the son of Prince Richard, is my kinsman and younger than I, more handsome than I am, equal to me in birth, wealth and power.[17]]

Melaz wisely accepts.

Orderic's story could be doubly inspired. On a Biblical level, Orderic compares Melaz to Bithiah, Pharoah's daughter, whom he says accompanied Moses and the Hebrews in safety when the Egyptians perished.

Marjorie Chibnall has noted that Orderic got this bit of information from a Biblical commentary that was incorrectly said to be by Saint Jerome (*Quaestiones hebraicae in libros Regum et Paralipomenon*).[18] Basing his story on I Chronicles 4:18, Pseudo Jerome gave the name Bithiah to the daughter of the Pharaoh whom he said rescued Moses, converted and married the Hebrew Mered. Orderic's comparison of the Biblical Hebrews and the Christian crusaders is in keeping with his overall plan of salvation history in his *Historia Ecclesiastica*.

Orderic's other inspiration could well have been the historical events of the veritable crusader Bohemond. An event in Orderic's account closely parallels Armenian sources of the crusade, thus there is reason to believe that he spoke to a reliable source for his story.[19] In both Orderic's story and the Armenian account, an exchange of captives takes place, and under Bohemond's command the Christians return the daughter of the emir of Antioch, Yaghi-Siyan. Orderic lightens the event by describing the princess as reluctantly returning to her people:

> Tunc Cassiani filia admiralii Antiochiae reddita est quae cum multo ploratu de carcere Christianorum extracta est. Quae cum interrogaretur quare ita fleret, respondit quod ideo sic ploraret, quia optimam porci carnem qua Christiani utuntur manducatura non esset.
>
> [At that time the daughter of Yaghi-Siyan, the emir of Antioch, was released, weeping bitterly as she was brought out of the Christian prison. When she was asked why she wept so, she replied that it was because in future she would not be able to eat the excellent pork that Christians eat.[20]]

While this last scene is almost too clever to be true, the concurrence of the story of Bohemond's capture, his eventual release, and even the minor detail of the return of the daughter of the emir is quite factual, and it is tempting to be lured along with Orderic into believing the story of Bohemond and Melaz to be true.

Nonetheless, it is less important that the story be true than that it rang true in the time that Orderic was writing. The thought of a Saracen princess aiding a French crusader and then marrying the son of a powerful French lord was not shocking. Remember as well that this is the first known European occurrence of this story, so we cannot simply say that Orderic and his compatriots believed the story because it was a commonly known fiction. For later generations, this would certainly be the case, as the examples of Saracen princesses aiding crusaders would continue to pile up. Perhaps in the history of Bohemond and Melaz we have the kernel of the event that would lead to the proliferation of a popular medieval love story.

Guibourc, the wife of Guillaume d'Orange, is probably the most remarkable Saracen princess of them all. Guillaume is the hero of an entire cycle of *gestes*, and he takes as his wife the Saracen Orable, who changes her name to Guibourc upon baptism. In one of the examples cited by C. Meredith

Jones, Orable enchants her first husband, Thibaut, in order to avoid consummating her marriage with him.[21] Thibaut finds himself turned into a small gold ball each night as he comes to bed with his wife. Yet Orable conserves her chastity by means of this enchantment, and that fact makes her a more suitable wife for Guillaume d'Orange. The story of Orable's marriage to Thibaut clearly captured the imagination of romance epic writers, who address her relationship to the hero with differing degrees of detail. One *chanson de geste* (*Chanson de Guillaume*) simply says that Guillaume takes her as his wife, stealing her from his Saracen enemy. Another tells of her action in the affair; the reader finds that Orable is in fact responsible for the release of Guillaume and his compatriots, who had been captured by her husband's men (*La Prise d'Orange*). Then, to buttress her suitability as wife of Guillaume, the story of Orable and Thibaut is told, as if to counter objections that Guillaume had married a woman who was no longer *pucele*.

These stories clarify that Orable was a suitable wife for Guillaume d'Orange. They show an interest in Orable/Guibourc (her baptismal name) surpassing that of any Christian-born woman in the *chansons de geste*. Clearly, after hearing the first story that mentioned Orable, the imagination of the audience was piqued and they wanted more stories about her and her giant-brother Rainouart. As each story raised new questions and new directions for the storytellers to explore, the history of Guibourc was written.

But at the same time that Guibourc is touted as a strong, supportive queen, other epics question her image. In some versions of *Aliscans*, *Le Moniage Guillaume* II, and *Foucon de Candie*, Guillaume tortured and killed two of Orable's children by Thibaut. While Orable is not the one to have perpetrated this horrible act, she could have refrained from marrying the murderer. In another text, a story where Orable evidently threw her infant son by Thibaut from the ramparts is said to exist.[22] These stories seem not to have been the more popular ones. They are omitted from the versions of the cycle that became codified and passed down as definitive. Nonetheless, the existence of a Medea-like image of Guibourc is troubling. The horror created when a mother kills a child is one that cannot be forgotten in the mind of the reader/listener. Just as the image of Medea as a child-killer has dominated her portrayal in modern interpretations of Greek mythology, so the story of Guilbourc having tossed her son to his death would have colored perceptions of Guilbourc as an ideal wife. Charles Knudson, while pointing out these odd variations on the Guibourc legend, does not propose an interpretation. He seems to feel that the legend of Guibourc as child-killer was simply a negative view of the Saracen that passed out of public realm after a few ill-received redactions.[23] However, this image is not unlike that of Exterminans, the monster of the *Beatus de Morgan* text mentioned in the opening of the chapter. Guibourc is an attractive and sensual woman at the same time that she betrays her first husband and kills their child. She is a woman literally capable of anything.

Focusing on the dubious side of literary Saracens like Guibourc, Sénac, in his book on the image of the Saracen, devotes only seven pages to "les femmes." According to his analysis, the female Saracen, or *sarassine*, is acceptable only as a mistress, concubine, slave, but not spouse.[24] Indeed, Orable must convert before she can marry. Like Bramimonde, the wife of Marsile in the *Chanson de Roland*, Orable's conversion leads to a new name and integration into Christian society. Sénac writes concerning the conversion of Bramimonde:

> En changeant de religion, elle se métamorphose : un nouveau nom lui est attribué. Le fossé a été franchi. Bramimonde chrétienne n'a plus d'intérĺt. Le silence peut la recouvrir. . . .[25]

While indeed that may be the case for Bramimonde, nothing could be further from the reaction to Orable's conversion to Guibourc. She remained in the medieval imagination, as the amplifications to her history prove. In later stories, she is referred to as "Dame Guibour," and she is admired and loved. This respect can only be due to her gutsy actions in her youth, as she saved the Christian crusaders and left her ineffectual husband Thibaut.

Leaving husbands and saving enemy troops are clearly achievements that the Christian woman had little opportunity to accomplish in the *chansons de geste*. As a literary figure, the Saracen woman therefore had a freedom from societal expectations that the Christian woman did not have. She could be a powerful woman in a text precisely because she was in reality already on the margins of society. The link between her liminal status and her power is manifest. Once she was successfully integrated into French society, she had to give up her (sexually) adventuresome ways. However, the stories of her glorious past always surrounded her. Her Saracen past was not something she had to live down, but rather the very foundation of her honor and prestige.

Contrary to Sénac's assertion, Guibourc's strength continues to enflame her husband, Guillaume, even after her conversion. In *Aliscans*, for example, Guillaume and his men are suffering great losses. Vivien, Guillaume's nephew, expires after a great battle, but takes the time to offer to his uncle a short praise of Guibourc, for whom he cares greatly. Guillaume decides to return to Orange to try to take refuge inside its walls. But Guibourc, still the keeper of impregnable tower, refuses to let her husband back into the city, claiming that she cannot recognize him as a vanquished soldier. Forced to return to the battlefield but encouraged by his wife's belief in his abilities, Guillaume manages to prove his honor by rescuing a group of captured Christians before returning to Orange. Her husband once again a hero in her eyes, now Guibourc will open the gates for Guillaume.

The desire on the part of some critics to read these women too negatively is easily understood. What is the modern reader to make of a Christian author who admires the wife of the Infidel? Sénac sees the presence of these women as a constant reproach to their Saracen husbands and menfolk, "le païen est inférieur à son épouse."[26] Even the positive qualities of the women can be read as tacit condemnation of the Saracen:

> Tout comme le gigantisme, la beauté sarrasine et la noblesse virile n'ont d'autres ambitions que de valoriser l'effort des chevaliers chrétiens et d'aviver l'attente d'une issue.[27]

A more satisfying explanation for the Western medieval fascination with the Saracen is that the Saracen could represent for the French listener many different things. It was a negative view, by all means, at times, but also positive at other moments, a view of the Saracen that reflected a very real admiration for their progress in arms and the arts. Saracen beauty was more than just a foil for Christian prowess. The desire and longing of epic and lyric translated into a tangible admiration for that which differed from the everyday. The Saracen could be both good and evil, beautiful and ugly, wise and foolish. Just because a character is seen to be negative at one moment does not imply that he or she will always be cast in that mold. The Saracen was remarkable, above all, for his or her ability to transform into whatever literary device the Christian author most needed. If a hideous renegade was called for, a Saracen fit the role. Likewise, if a model of courtliness and chivalry was on the menu, the Saracen filled the part superbly.

The powerful Saracen princess managed to mirror her Christian sister admirably. She served as the powerful woman that Christian authors were hesitant to put into their works. Since the Saracen was already marginal, depictions of the *sarrasine* wielding great power over her menfolk did not provoke negative reactions. The storyteller could express admiration for a strong woman without entering into the questions of female power that were current in Christendom at that time.

Twelfth-century Europe saw for the first time a fierce battle to authenticate female power in the absence of a male monarch. Henry I asked for and received the support of his barons to enthrone his daughter, the Empress Maud, for lack of any suitable male heir. After his death, however, pledges of support were rescinded and Maud's power was upheld only through years of fighting. The royal lineage passed through her to her son, Henry II, who married Eleanor of Aquitaine. Eleanor inherited the large and strategically important Aquitaine, which she managed to take with her in first marriage to Louis VII and which reverted to her when their marriage was dissolved. The question of female rule and its validity was thus of utmost importance at the time of the *chansons de geste*.

Other women also exercised power over land at this epoch. The Crusades took men away from their estates for extended periods of time, and women gained respect by handling the affairs of their estates. Margaret Ker compares the benefits reaped by women during the Crusades to those of certain Western women during World War I.[28] During this period, strong regional houses developed their own vertical lineage independent of the French crown, passing down power, wealth, lands and prestige. As Eleanor and

Maud among others illustrate, in cases where there were no male heirs, women obtained and successfully defended their inheritance. Anderson and Zinsser note that "In part, the English and French families controlled so much land because they relied on their women as trusted surrogates."[29]

Furthermore, the nobility did not have a monopoly on strong women. Legal records from the time show that women were enjoying independent, decision-making roles such as "femmes du peuple médecins" and "maîtresses d'artisanat."[30] Religious mysticism and female monastic orders gave women alternatives to or at least some alleviation from the patriarchy. Marriage became a sacrament,[31] and the twelfth-century witnessed the blossoming of the Cult of Mary accompanied by the explosion in the number of cathedrals dedicated to the mother of Jesus.[32] Anderson and Zinsser comment on the importance of the religious aspect: "In the twelfth and thirteenth centuries and again in the sixteenth and seventeenth centuries, women knew the exhilaration of the 'equality of all believers,' could forget distinctions of nature and function, and embrace forbidden roles and activities in the name of the revitalized Christian faith."[33]

But this power did not go uncontested. As R. Howard Bloch and others have shown,[34] writers like William IX of Aquitaine and Chrétien de Troyes questioned the model of female power through their use of courtly lyric and literature. The woman on a pedestal could not be a threat. The writers of the *chansons de geste* do not participate in this putting of the woman on a pedestal. The Saracen women are women of action, as well as great beauty. They set their sights on a goal and accomplish it. They far outstrip the men in resourcefulness. Telling their stories in courts provided models for active, ruling women. These are the women who would be appreciated by the ruling women in the courts of the South. Guibourc is more like Eleanor of Aquitaine than any of the disappearing, self-effacing beauties of courtly literature. The link between the two women is made all the more poignant when taking into account Eleanor's reputed unrestrained sexual activity while on crusade and her eventual remarriage to Henry. Guibourc and Eleanor control the political destinies of their people just as they take control of their own sexuality.

The similarity between Saracens and Christians is echoed in descriptions of the women. They are most often described as "blanche a la char comme est la flor d'espine."[35] Their whiteness signifies their beauty and also their potential for integration into French society. For all purposes, they could be French women, as they fit the aesthetic mold. The whiteness of their skin does not reflect a historical circumstance of Christian encounters with light-skinned Saracens. Saracens are in general portrayed as black, and the light-skinned French are unable to hide among them as spies. As Bueves sends out some of his men to get reinforcements in the *Siege de Barbastre*, he is concerned about their ability to passes through enemy lines. He voices his reservation:

> Mes une seule chose si me fait trepanser:
> Que vos estes si blanc et voz vis bel et cler.
> Si ne gart onques l'heure que vos face afoler,
> L'amirant et si dru, s'il vos puent trover.
> Que tres par mi lor ost vos covient a paser.³⁶
>
> [But only one thing makes me hesitate greatly. You are very white and your face handsome and light. I don't doubt a bit that the Amirant and his men would have you killed if they could find you, for you will have to go right through the middle of their troops.]

An ointment is used to blacken their skin, and they pass through without being taken. Upon arrival, however, they have difficulty convincing King Louis that they are messengers from the French. Louis retorts:

> Fil a putain ! paien, chetif maleüré !
> Ou avez la mençonge ne pris ne contrové? . . .
> Et vos estes si noir comme airement triblé.³⁷
>
> [Son of a bitch! Miserable pagan prisoner! Where did you get or invent the lie? You are as black as well-mixed ink.]

The disguised men are saved by the application of some vinegar that returns them to their very white selves.

So the whiteness of some of the Saracen women cannot be read as a realistic portrayal of the medieval French view of the Saracen body. Rather, it illustrates desire on the part of the male authors of the texts. The object of the medieval equivalent of locker-room banter, Malatrie is described in the *Siege de Barbastre*:

> Et dit li un a l'autre: " Ou fu ceste trovee?
> N'est pas chose terrestre, ainz est chose faee.
> Molt puet avoir grant joie dedenz son cuer posee,
> Ne puet estre encombré cil qui l'a espousee
> a nul jor de sa vie."³⁸
>
> [The one man said to the other, "Where did you find her? She is not an earthly thing, truly she is an otherwordly thing. He who marries her can have great joy in his heart, for he who marries her will never be uncomfortable a single day of his life.]

The beautiful, white Saracen woman is thus rendered both a "chose" and a "faee." She is otherwordly, and her husband (unlike husbands of all other women, we are to understand) would never tire of her.

These white Saracens should be contrasted with the black ones, the equally otherworldly anti-heroines found in *Fierabras* and *Aliscans*. In *Fierabras*, the Christian kills the giant Saracen, but he has a redoubtable wife:

> Ce est une gaiande plus noire que pevrée;
> Grant ot la fourcéure et le geule avoit lée
> Et si avoit de haut une lance levée,
> Les ex avoit plus rouges que n'est flambe alumée;
> Moult est de tout en tout laide et deffigurée.

> [She was a giant blacker than pepper; with great hips and a wide mouth; with the height of an upright lance, her eyes were redder than a lighted torch; she is utterly ugly and disfigured.[39]]

The giantess Flohart in *Aliscans* is a frightening double of this woman:

> .XV. piez ot, tant l'ont François esmee;
> D'un cuir de bugle estoit envelopee;[40]
> ...De sa bouche ist une si grant fumee,
> Trestote l'ost en fu empullentee.[41]
> ...Et Flohart a la ventaille saisie,
> As dent li a del hauberc esrachie,
> Ausi tranglot come ce fust formagie.[42]

> [She was 15 feet tall, and as such the French were terrified of her. She was wrapped in the skin of a buffalo; From her mouth issued a great fiery smoke, so that the troops were immediately burned alive. Flohart grabbed the ventail and tore his hauberk from him with her teeth. And then she devoured him like he was cheese.]

Here is the negative side of the image of the Saracen woman. When the Saracen woman decides to stay with her man, as the two monstrous women above choose to do, they can no longer be considered salvageable. They become danger personified. They are "sur-déterminé de l'extérieur," a phrase Frantz Fanon uses to describe the black person.[43] No longer even human, these voracious giants are more threatening to the French soldiers than any army of Saracen men. Like the mother of Beowulf, their maternal and wifely instincts are intimately connected with perversions of the body and excesses of violence. Their monstrous and fire-breathing bodies are designed to protect their brood. They, unlike white Saracen women, are meant to stay with their families and eventually perish at the hands of the French crusaders.

These women, like other medieval women in the anitfeminist discourse of the French Middle Ages, are defined by their two orifices: their vaginas and their mouths. Their gaping maws, humorously depicted as Flohart tears off a crusader's hauberk and eats him as if he were cheese, are omnivorous, fire-producing vaginas looking for men to devour. These Saracen women fall into E. Jane Burns' definition of the typical medieval characterization of the libidinous woman; "Impossible to satisfy, always demanding more sex as she often seeks more money or more food, this woman simply cannot ever get enough of her 'man'."⁴⁴ Here, the Saracen woman literally enacts the male fear of being "eaten up."

The mouth/vagina connection is found as well in the oversexed white Saracen, like Orable, who is holed up in Gloriete, her tower of love. Other Saracen princesses "eat up" their French crusaders; in the *Siege de Barbastre* a young Saracen princess is warned that she will be ravished if the French catch her so she immediately goes to offer herself to one of the French soldiers. In the same epic poem, Gerart kisses his beloved Saracen princess, Malatrie, but he avoids her mouth "because she is pagan":

> Plus de .XX. fois la besse en .i. tenant,
> El menton, en la face, qu'elle avoit bel et gent.
> Pour sou qu'elle est paiene va sa bouche eschivant.⁴⁵
>
> [More than twenty times he kisses her while holding her, on her chin, on her face, which were lovely and noble. Because she is a pagan he avoids her mouth.]

The sexuality that surpasses the limits of the female body can either destroy, as the black Saracen women illustrate, or lead to the founding of a noble line, as seen in the couple of Guibourc and Guillaume. Whereas French soldiers are terrified of the black women, they find the sexuality of the white women enticing. However, the white body represents a considerable danger for the French man. Guillaume's spies report to him:

> Et dame Orable, une roïne gente,
> Il n'a si bele desi en Orïente,
> Bel a le cors, eschevie est et gente,
> Blanche la char comme la flor en l'ente.
> Dex ! mar i fu ses cors et sa jovente,
> Quant Dex ne croit, le pere omnipotente!⁴⁶
>
> [And Lady Orable, a noble queen, there is not one so beautiful from here to the Orient. She has a beautiful body, elegant and noble. Her skin is as white as the flower in bloom. God! May her body and youth be cursed, for she does not believe in God, the almighty father!]

Other spies and friends of Guillaume repeat this refrain, and all try to convince him of the folly of his double obsession for Orable and the city of Orange.

Orable's status as dangerous woman, loose cannon, is underlined as Guillaume speaks with her relative, the King of Aragon. Having entered Orange disguised as an interpreter for the absent Thibaut, husband of Orable, Guillaume asks about the queen. The King of Aragon has some very definite opinions about the woman he is charged with protecting:

New Songs with New Rhythms: The Romance Epic   49

> . . . " Il (Thibaut) fet mout grant folie,
> Quar il est vielz, s'a la barbe florie,
> Et ceste est bele et juenete meschine,
> Il n'a tant bele en tote paiennie.
> En Glorïete mainne ses drüeries;
> Mielz ameroit...Sorbant de Venice,
> Un bacheler juene de barbe prime,
> Qui de deport et d'armes set bien vivre,
> Qu'el ne feroit Tiebaut d'Esclavonie.
> Trop par est fox vielz hom qu'aime meschine,
> Tost en est cous et tornez a folie."
> Ot le Guillelmes, si commença a rire :
> " Voir, dit Guillelmes, or ne l'amez vos mie ?
> —Ge non, por voir, Damedex la maudie !
> Ge vorroie ore qu'ele fust en Aufrique
> Ou a Baudas, el regne d'Aumerie."⁴⁷

["Thibaut did a really silly thing, for he is old and has a white beard, and she is a beautiful and young girl. There is none so beautiful in all the pagan lands. In Gloriette she carries on her love affairs. She would prefer...Sorbant of Venice, a young bachelor with a dark beard, who knows well how to lead the life of joy and arms, than she would Thibaut of Esclavonia. An old man who loves a young lady is too silly; soon he is tricked and driven mad." Guillaume heard this and began to laugh. "Truly," said Guillaume, "you don't like her a bit?" "No, I don't, it's true, may God curse her! I would rather see her in Africa or in Baudas, in the kingdom of Aumerie."]

Orable's reputation does not seem to bother Guillaume. If anything, he is more attracted to her than ever before. The seductress, beautiful but dangerous Orable, is not seen as an inappropriate consort for Guillaume. Both are young, comely, and adventuresome. Excepting her religion, Orable is an ideal mate for Guillaume.

In contrast, from the outset it is clear that Flohart will never be integrated into French society, whereas the beautiful Orable has every sign of making a suitable wife. The inconceivable conversion of the black women, impossible because of their fidelity to their people, is reflected in the blackness of their skin. Though Orable's brother, the giant Rainouart, is Christianized and lauded for his prowess on the battlefield, the female equivalent of the converted Saracen giant does not exist. The Saracen woman can be strong, but if she is to be accepted in French society, she must also be beautiful and, above all perhaps, white.

The translation movement led to an increased interest in new relationships with Saracens. The epic relationship epitomized in the *Chanson de Roland* offered little in the way of cultural integration. Likewise, the emphasis on inability to communicate found in troubadour poetry left little room for interchange. An optimism following the translation movement indicated that other types of relationship could be formed, but the existing genres did not quite suffice for describing newer possibilities. Medieval authors, looking for ways to demonstrate both difference and similarity found the romance epic to be a genre that allowed for creative expansion. A hybrid itself, the romance epic is both epic, with warfare a central concern, and romance, a narrative generally including one or more love intrigues. This hybridism is at the very heart of the text, as Sharon Kinoshita writes of the *Prise d'Orange*:

> Derided for its lack of narrative coherence, celebrated for its comic inversion of epic motifs, [it] functions not in spite of its crossing of discourses and genres but because of it.[48]

Earlier critics of the epic romance considered that the genre was invented for women, as they grew more powerful in the courts of France and demanded entertainment more interesting than the battle stories, considered to be men's stories. However, having considered the ambivalent nature of the roles of women in the romance epic, it seems clear that it can no longer be viewed as simply a story to appeal to the ladies of the court. These romance epics had as their goal not an effort to appease female listeners, but rather a new way of getting at the social conundrum produced by changing relationships between Christians and Muslims. Saracen women became the site of cultural appropriation for French men. Just as Peter the Venerable wanted to understand the Koran to better overcome the heresy of Islam, so medieval authors forged fictive relationships with Muslims to appropriate and conquer another culture.

If epic sought to destroy and lyric denied communication, the romance epic proffered a third alternative—cultural assimilation. The white Saracen woman, so very French in her appearance, could become both Saracen and French in this hybrid genre. The Saracen male warrior could also become French, guarding his physical difference but otherwise bowing to French cultural superiority. The romance epic represents at times a high point in belief in the possibility of overcoming and enfolding the Saracen, but the fantastic, magical elements, combined with unrealistic physical portraits, betray the author, showing that he or she continues to depict the impossible.

NOTES

1. Ngugi wa Thiong'o, Homecoming: Essays (London: Heinemann, 1972), p. 30.
2. Philippe Sénac, *L'image de l'autre: histoire de l'occident médiéval face à Islam* (Paris: Flammarion, 1983) p. 34.
3. Gabrielle M. Spiegel, *Romancing the Past: the rise of vernacular prose historiography in 13th-century France* (Berkeley: UCP, 1993), p. 5.

4. Sénac, op. cit., p. 81.

5. Marie-Thérèse d'Alverny, *La connaissance de l'Islam dans l'Occident médiéval* (Brookfield, Vt: Variorum, 1994), p. 70.

6. "Et ut nichil dampnabilis sectae nostros lateret, totam illam illorum legem, quam in propria lingua Alkoran vel Alkyren uocant, ex integro et per ordinem feci transferri." Giles Constable, ed. *The Letters of Peter the Venerable* (Cambridge, MA: Harvard University Press, 1967), Letter 111, p. 295.

7. C. Meredith Jones, "The Conventional Saracen of the Songs of Geste," *Speculum* 17 (1942), p. 225.

8. *Aliscans*, ed. C. Régnier. 2 vols (Paris: Champion, 1990), lines 1256–59.

9. Ibid., lines 79–80.

10. See F.M. Warren, "The Enamoured Saracen Princess in Orderic Vital and the French Epic," PMLA 29 (1914), pp. 341–58; and Philip Bennett, "The Storming of the Other World, the Enamoured Muslim Princess and the Evolution of the Legend of Guillaume d'Orange," *Guillaume d'Orange and the Chanson de geste, Reading: Société Rencesvals*, ed. Wolfgang Emden. (Reading: Société Rencesvals,1984), pp. 1–14; Charles A. Knudson, "Le thème de la princesse sarrasine dans La Prise d'Orange," *Romance Philology* XXII (4) (1969), pp. 449–462. Several articles came out of a Société Rencesvals meeting that pertain to women in epic: Kimberlee Anne Campbell, "Fighting Back: a survey of patterns of female agressiveness in the Old French chansons de geste," Sarah Kay, "La représentation de la féminité dans les chansons de geste," Hans-Erich Keller, "La belle Sarrasine dans Fierabras et ses dérivés," William W. Kibler, "Les personnages féminins dans la geste de Nanteuil," Jean-Claude Vallecalle, "Rupture et intégration: l'héroïne révoltée dans les chansons de geste," in *Charlemagne in the North*, ed. Philip Bennett, Anne E. Cobby and Graham Runnalls (Edinburgh: Société Rencesvals, 1993). See also Sarah Kay, *The Chansons de Geste in the Age of Romance* (Oxford: Clarendon Press, 1995).

11. Jones, op. cit., p. 218.

12. I argue elsewhere that the inimitable qualities of the Saracen woman function to contain the power of contemporary Western women. See Lynn Tarte Ramey, "Role Models? Saracen Women in Medieval French Epic," *Romance Notes*, forthcoming.

13. Joseph Bédier, "La Composition de la Chanson de Fierabras," *Romania* 17 (1888), p. 48.

14. F. M. Warren, "The Enamoured Saracen Princess in Orderic Vital and the French Epic," PMLA 28 (1914), p. 347.

15. M. Winterbottom, trans., *The Elder Seneca Declamations in Two Volumes* (Cambridge: Harvard University Press, 1974), p. 135.

16. Marjorie Chibnall, trans., *Orderic Vital's Ecclesiastical History* (Oxford: Clarendon Press, 1968–80), p. V, 258–9.

17. Ibid., pp. 378–9.

18. Ibid., p. 378. See Migne, PL, 23,1372 for Pseudo-Jerome text.

19. Warren has proposed that Orderic may have spoken to Bohemond himself, op. cit., p. 355.

20. Chibnall, op. cit., pp. 372–3.

21. See *Enfances Guillaume*, ed. P. Henry, (Paris: Champion, 1935).
22. This problem was first explored by Knudson, op. cit., p. 456.
23. Ibid., p. 457.
24. Sénac, op. cit., p. 93.
25. Ibid., p. 92.
26. Ibid., p. 91.
27. Ibid., p. 78.
28. Margaret Ker, "Women in Medieval Society" *Exploring Women's Past*, Patrica Crawford, ed. (Sydney: George Allen & Unwin, 1983), p. 35.
29. Bonnie S. Anderson and Judith P. Zinsser, A *History of Their Own*, Vol. I (New York: Harper and Row, 1988), p. 277.
30. Thérèse B. Lynn, "Pour une réhabilitation d'Eve," *The French Review* 48 (1975), p. 872.
31. Ker, op. cit., p. 29.
32. Lynn, op. cit., p. 872.
33. Anderson, op. cit., p. 182.
34. R. Howard Bloch, *Medieval Misogyny* (Chicago: University of Chicago Press, 1991).
35. Orable, as portrayed in *La Prise d'Orange: Chanson de geste de la fin du XIIe siÈcle*, ed. Claude Régnier (Paris: …ditions Klincksieck, 1972), line 279.
36. *Le Siège de Barbastre*, ed. J.L. Perrier (Paris: Champion, 1926), lines 3237–3241.
37. Ibid., lines 3459–67.
38. Ibid., lines 7234–7.
39. Passage and translation taken from Jacqueline de Weever, *Sheba's Daughters: Whitening and Demonizing the Saracen Woman in Medieval French Epic* (New York: Garland, 1998), p. 220. De Weever refers to the 1860 edition of *Fierabras*, edited by A. Kroeber and G. Servois. Both editions of the text are extremely difficult to find.
40. *Aliscans*, ed. C. Régnier, 2 vols (Paris: Champion, 1990), lines 6721–22.
41. Ibid., lines 6731–32.
42. Ibid., lines 6767–69.
43. Frantz Fanon, *Les damnés de la terre* (Paris: Gallimard, 1991), p. 95.
44. E. Jane Burns, *Bodytalk* (Philadelphia: University of Pennsylvania Press, 1993), p. 51.
45. Raymond Weeks, "The Siège de Barbastre," *Romanic Review* 10 (4) (1919), p. 318.
46. *La Prise d'Orange*, op. cit., lines 202–7.
47. Ibid., lines 619–34.
48. Sharon Kinoshita, "The Politics of Courtly Love:: *La Prise d'Orange* and the Conversion of the Saracen Queen," *Romanic Review* 82 (2) (1995), p. 285.

5. Forging Relationships: Law, "History," and National Identity

Twenty-five years before the *chanson de geste*, *Le Siege de Barbastre*, was written, a revolution in church or canon law was taking place in Bologna and Paris. The mid-twelfth century saw the work of two jurists, Gratian of Bologna, whose *Decretum* appeared in 1140,[1] and Peter Lombard of Paris, whose *Sententiae* were promulgated a decade later. The two men wrote extensively on questions of canon law, and in particular, on the question of marriage, as Georges Duby documents in *The Knight, the Lady and the Priest*. Ecclesiastical courts had addressed what constitutes a legal marriage for centuries without codification. Due to the mixing of Germanic customs (*coutumier*, or custon law), Roman law, and the teachings of the Bible, conflicting views on legal marriage had been set forth. Gratian is accredited with the first systematic redaction of canon law as he reconciled the different rulings which had been made by ecclesiastical courts over the centuries. Peter Lombard reexamined the case of marriage, and his work inspired theologians to debate the newly established sacrament of marriage. Around their teachings grew up schools of thought devoted to the ideas of each man. Thus, at the time of the writing of the *Siege de Barbastre*, the work of Gratian and Lombard formed a significant part of informed discussion all over medieval Western Europe.

Jean Gaudemet reports that a literature of "questions" on marriage arose during the late twelfth century, telling of one of the *disputationes* at Oxford that explored a sticky case of divorce and kinship.[2] While the Old French *chanson de geste*, the *Siege de Barbastre*, is not technically a part of this literature, it too explores the legal aspect of interethnic marriage. Close reading of the *Siege de Barbastre* and examination of the historical context of the tale place it within the late twelfth-century preoccupation with marriage. The link between canon law and captivity in the Old French *Siege de Barbastre* illustrates the bind encountered when incorporating the Other into Christian society.

The story of the siege of Barbastro is historically attested. In 1064 a group of Norman Christians invaded Spain and besieged the Muslim-held city of Barbastro, leading off the Muslim women who would later appear in William IX's court. Le *Siege de Barbastre*, the *chanson de geste*, was written about 100 years after the actual siege and through its title bears homage to this momentous event. However, many of the historical events are altered. The siege reverses the position of the forces, placing the French inside the walls of Barbastro and the Muslims attacking from the outside. There is no slaughter of innocent persons. The heroes of the chansons de geste—King Louis and Bueves de Commarcis—replace historical knights. One major similarity remains, however—the focus on capture. The ultimately static situation of the siege is peppered with small battle scenes where captives are taken or rescued. The story is framed by the capture of a married French woman at the beginning and the marriage of a Muslim captive to a French hero at the end. The number of Muslim women acquired by the French in this *chanson de geste* is four rather than the five thousand in the chronicles, but their presence indicates both knowledge of the capture of women at Barbastro in 1064 and an intense interest in the relationship between captivity and conjugal life.

The commonplace occurrence of kidnapping or taking by force the daughter of the enemy ruler was a preoccupation in Roman and early Christian times.[3] Raptus, the kidnapping of a woman usually accompanied by forced intercourse, was treated as stepping stone to marriage by Germanic law codes and even the Bible. The man who carried off the woman was expected to marry her. Exodus 22:16-17 states:

> If a man seduces a virgin who is not betrothed, and lies with her, he shall give the marriage present for her, and make her his wife. If her father utterly refuses to give her to him, he shall pay money equivalent to the marriage present for virgins.

Likewise, the *Usatges de Barcelona*, a secular law text from the mid-twelfth century, shows that this view of raptus was still quite common in parts of medieval Europe. The *Usatges* state:

> If anyone violently corrupts a virgin, he shall either marry her if she and her parents wish and give her dowry, or he shall give her a husband of her worth.[4]

Roman law, however, forbids such marriages and death was usually the fate of the raptor. Carrying off an unmarried woman was a most serious crime; the twelfth-century canonists do not prescribe death for the perpetrator, but both Lombard and Gratian refuse to validate marriage by raptus. The late twelfth-century *chansons de geste* reflect the canonist position, with raptus being a commonplace event that does not guarantee marriage but in fact often does lead to marriage.

Raptus is a central issue in the *Siege de Barbastre*: five women are carried off by enemy troops. The first is the countess Hermenjart, wife of Aymeri de Narbonne, whose capture starts off the conflict between pagans and Christians. She calls out as she is carried off:

> Aymeri, secor moi, por amor Deu le grant! . . .
> Or me randront paien ici a l'amirant,
> Et fera de mon cors trestout a son talant;
> Reprovier i avront li pere et li enfant,
> Et ge serai honnie.[5]

> [Aymeri, save me for the love of God! . . . These pagans will hand me over to the amirant, and he will have his way with my body; The father and son will be blamed for it, and I will be humiliated.]

Raptus would lead to physical violation and symbolize the defeat of the French. Hermanjart is soon rescued and placed in the safest part of the castle, the *donjon*, to wait out the siege. Unlike the Saracen princess, the French matron will never encounter the enemy within her own walls. Her safety is the central concern of the troops, and whenever the question of surrender is raised, her capture is a main objection. The physical possession of the women of the French would mean their total defeat.

The next woman to be captured is Malatrie, the beautiful daughter of the Saracen leader. Through hearing of the valiant fighting of the French soldiers, she falls in love with Girart. Malatrie, unlike Hermenjart, wishes to be captured. Betrothed by her father to a Saracen knight, she entices her fiancé to take her on a ride near the city, and they are predictably set upon by French knights. Girart unhorses the Saracen, and goes to meet Malatrie. She, upon hearing his name, announces:

> Girart, car m'en portez, franc chevalier oneste.
> Por la teue amistié creré en la paterne,
> Si serai crestïenne, bautisisee et converte.[6]

> [Girart, take me with you, frank and honest knight. For your love, I will believe in God the Father, and so I will become Christian, baptized and converted.]

She literally asks to be taken captive. Her cooperation is crucial, for since she requests it, her "kidnapping" could not be construed in any way to require the Frenchman to marry her. Malatrie's willingness to convert prepares the way for an eventual, consensual marriage between her and Girart. As if answering the canonists Gratian and Lombard, the author of the *Siege de Barbastre* shows that the marriage between the two lovers is not based on physical force and kidnapping.

The final scene of raptus involves three young noblewomen who come with the Saracen reinforcements for the siege. These young women, like Malatrie, are intrigued by stories they hear of the Franco-Norman knights. They are told:

> Et dus Bueves ses peres nos toli Malatrie,
> La fille l'amustant de Cordres la garnie.
> Mes sachiez une chose, droiz est que le vos die;
> S'il vos püent sessir, que tost seroiz ravie.[7]
>
> [Bueves took from us, her people, Malatrie, the daughter of the amustant of the rich city of Cordres. You should know something, and it is right that I should tell you, that if they are able to take you, you will soon be ravished.]

Rather than causing fear, this warning provokes the three women to do all that they can to attract the attention of the young French warriors. Once again, raptus is not seen as the crime that Roman law and the canonists denounced but as a reward. They send a messenger telling the men to come and visit their tent. The French men come, and while they are in bed with the women, the Saracens attack, led by the father of one of the women. The men barely escape but the girls are retaken by the Saracens. They claim that they were taken by force,[8] which in canon law would eliminate their responsibility. The play between the condemned act of rape and the desire of the women to be taken by the Frenchmen shows a rather ironic view of the newly codified Church position against raptus. The Saracen women want to be snatched, ravished, and, eventually, possessed in marriage.

Opposed to the old views of marriage contracted by physical possession of the woman, both Gratian and Lombard agree that consent is the basis of all marriages. Here the author introduces his twist. A definite focus on consent in the *chanson de geste* is illustrated as King Louis comes to Malatrie, saying:

> Bele, ce dit li rois, est Girarz vostre amis?
> Volez le vos avoir? Si sera vo mariz.[9]
>
> [Beautiful one, is Girart your lover? Do you wish to have him? If so, you will be married.]

With her consent, she underscores her attraction to Girart and nullifies any complaint that she might have been taken from her people by force. A kidnapping/rape that was consensual could not be considered either kidnapping or rape in the medieval author's code. The author calls into question the captivity of the original, historical women of Barbastro. They, like Malatrie and her sisters, must enjoy being in the hands of the French. Their kidnapping and rape (as can be imagined must have occurred) reflect not the misdeeds of the French, but the fulfillment of the wishes of all Saracen women.

The consent of Girart and Malatrie is obtained, but they are not yet considered married. There is an obstacle in that Malatrie remains a pagan. The absolute insistence on her conversion, though not surprising, is a twelfth-century phenomenon. In the early years of the Christian church, Paul had dealt with this issue. He warned Christians not to marry pagans, writing:

> Do not be mismated with unbelievers. For what partnership have righteousness and iniquity? Or what fellowship has light with darkness? (2 Corinthians 6:14).

However, interfaith marriages were not at that time considered invalid. Paul also penned:

> To the rest I say, not the Lord, that if any brother has a wife who is an unbeliever, and she consents to live with him, he should not divorce her. If any woman has a husband who is an unbeliever, and he consents to live with her, she should not divorce him. For the unbelieving husband is consecrated through his wife, and the unbelieving wife is consecrated through her husband. Otherwise, your children would be unclean, but as it is they are holy. (I Corinthians 7:12-14)

Church fathers, including Augustine,[10] agreed with the relatively tolerant position of Paul. From as early as the fourth century, local councils spoke out against marriages between infidels and Christians, but once such marriages were contracted, they were not invalidated. Contrary to the Church fathers, Lombard and Gratian both agreed that a marriage with an infidel, someone who had not been baptized, was considered null and void.[11] Not only were Christians discouraged from marrying pagans, when such marriages did take place, they were not considered legitimate. Conversion became absolutely essential to legitimate marriage. This twelfth-century view of marriage exhibits itself in fiction, as Malatrie must be baptised before her marriage to a Christian. Not only does the Saracen woman wish to belong to the French soldier, she also desires in her heart of hearts to be Christian.

Society accepts her into the fold. Consent of the parents and secular authorities, a major element in both Roman law and the Frankish customs, was deemed unnecessary by Gratian and Lombard. Although by canon law the approval of the king is in no way required for a marriage to take place, Louis calls Girart to him and says:

> Girart, dit Looïs, tenez ceste mollier.
> Et Girarz la reçoit . . .[12]

> [Girart, take this woman, and Girart takes her and kissed her three times.]

With King Louis' approval, the marriage between Christian and (former) Saracen is officially deemed appropriate and positive. The king's approval of Malatrie's marriage to Girart illustrates what has been described as a gradual reduction in the power of the secular courts from the tenth to twelfth centuries in the case of marriage.[13] Ecclesiastical courts and decrees became the bases for legitimizing and legislating marriages. However, when questions of legitimacy of marriage became wrapped up in questions of succession, the secular courts reasserted themselves and won out over the ecclesiastical courts.[14] In this case, Malatrie is quite a catch for Girart. Louis states that he knows of no girl who is a better catch from Barbastro to Paris:

> Molt estes preuz et sage, dit le rois Looïs;
> Ne quit melz dotrinee deci jusq'a Paris.[15]
>
> [You are very noble and wise, said King Louis. I don't know of any better educated from here to Paris.]

Because of the land and power Malatrie will confer upon Girart, the blessing of the king is essential for the marriage to take place. The marriage of Girart and Malatrie shows a politic view of societal consent to marriage. The King's approval unites the two lovers; such approval is both socially convenient and conforms to the chivalric ideal. As Gratian and Lombard had found that only the consent of the two to be married is essential to form a union, the approval of the king would not technically be required, but the *chanson de geste* shows that in cases where succession is involved, approval was likely to be sought. Parental consent, however, is virtually absent. Malatrie's father has been converted and his gifts indicate that he approves of the marriage, but he is not asked his opinion concerning the marriage. When the Saracen woman is integrated into French society, her ties to the French replace even blood ties to her people.

A final twelfth-century view of marriage is revealed as vows are made. The couple exchanges crowns and rings and Louis blesses them again. However, they are not pronounced married until Louis' chaplain, Richier, marries them.[16] Pope Alexander III, a contemporary of the author of the Siege de Barbastre, insisted upon the presence of a priest at marriages. The *Siege de Barbastre* therefore illustrates an idealized twelfth-century marriage. Both parties are Christians who agree to marry. Their union brings great riches and land to an extremely valiant but landless knight. The secular authorities, in the form of King Louis, as well as the ecclesiastical authorities, in the form of Louis' chaplain, bless the union. Their vows are made in public, in front of a priest. Thus the marriage of Malatrie and Girart combines the canonists' view of marriage with a chivalric ideal.

The historical story of Barbastro was far from the idealized picture painted in the *chanson de geste*. The Normans held Barbastro for less than a year; Muslim forces reconquered the city in 1065. The story of the capture of Barbastro did not fail to ignite the imagination of those who heard about it; the immense riches of the city and the decadent lifestyle of the conquering Normans related by chronicler Amatus of Montecassino could provide endless stories. The Muslim captives living in Christian lands would also serve as a constant reminder of the battle. The Spanish law code, *Las Siete Partidas*, of the thirteenth century deals with Christians captured by Moors, indicating that such occurrences were either commonplace or had entered into the imagination of the period. On the question of inheritance, the code states:

There remains a further way in which ancient authorities held that the child could inherit his father's property. This is when the [Christian] man who is held captive comes to believe that those at home who should be trying to secure his release are not making any effort to do so, and he in his desperation to be free has a child by some woman of the [Muslim] faith who promises to help him to freedom: if after such a promise she manages to achieve this, and comes home with the man, the son or daughter accompanying her or without her [has a right to the inheritance].[17]

Here the Siete Partidas reads like a plot line for a *chanson de geste*. Sieges on Muslim-held lands feature prominently in twelfth-century *chansons de geste*, and the topos of a Muslim woman being taken off to Christian lands is attested in over seventeen different *chansons de geste*. Like the *Siege de Barbastre*, the other *chansons de geste* are barely concerned with historical events. Many focus on captivity and marriage, and this emphasis is not incidental. The proliferation of chansons de geste in the late twelfth century coincides with the codification of marriage laws and the firming up of Church rulings. Marriage, perhaps the most important element of the social structure, is continually examined by these *chansons de geste*.

James Muldoon in *Popes, Lawyers and Infidels* notes that Gratian's *Decretum* deals only briefly with interfaith marriage. Muldoon feels that this reflects the state of Christian-infidel relations in the mid-twelfth century. Since the crusades had barely begun, he writes, the *Decretum* did not devote much attention to the status of the infidel. Surely this view is insufficient in accounting for the large amount of contact between Muslims and Christians that had already taken place by the time Gratian and Lombard were writing. Indeed, the canonists do not deal sufficiently with the changing social scene, and Christians were left with little direction for interpreting their intimate involvement with infidels. The *chansons de geste* could well have been the space where Christians explored for themselves the different roles of the Saracen and the relationships that could be forged with them. The stories provide scenarios in which the newly forming doctrines can be tested out and examined.

The *Siege de Barbastre* shows concern with the issues of interfaith marriage, raptus, and consent of the parties, parents and overlords—as do many other romance epics of the period. The captive women in the historical siege of Barbastro provide not only a good story for the jongleurs to tell but also the impetus to create stories about interfaith relations and marriage prospects. These stories work out contemporary problems of cultural interaction and societal ceremony. Captivity, a socially current topic during the Crusades, intersects with marriage as medieval writers exploit topics relevant to their audiences. Killing and raptus are transformed into marriage and consent. The siege that happened 100 years before could not be told as it really happened, for the relationships between Christians and Muslim were no longer so bent on destruction. Thus, the retelling of the massacre at Barbastro as the courtship and marriage of two persons of different faiths seems oddly appropriate.

Starting with the *Chanson de Roland* and continuing in the *chansons de geste* of the twelfth and thirteenth centuries, medieval French writers sought to establish the origins of their country in the legend of Charlemagne, who represented so many different things to the national consciousness. Charlemagne was depicted in terms that could provoke comparison with other great founders of nations before him. Stories that were told about him did not require factual veracity. More importantly, tales needed to invoke images of other figures that commanded respect. Christ and King David were natural inspirations for Charlemagne's portrait. Like Christ, Charlemagne had twelve close followers, his "douze pairs." Ganelon, a Judas figure, betrayed Charlemagne and his men for money, according to some sources. Like King David, who was the model for Christ, Charlemagne fought to keep his people, the people of God, free from the yoke of the Infidel. With legendary strength and resolve, Charlemagne saved the French time and again from the Saracen threat. But the crown was also a burden, as David experienced, and the closing *laisses* of the *Chanson de Roland* invoke the never-ending battle of the leader of God's people against the enemies of the faith.

This integral part of Charlemagne's image, that of the defender of the faith, makes the stories that grew up around him all the more curious. In *Mainet*,[18] which tells the story of Charlemagne's youth, as David was banished from court under King Saul, so young Charlot was chased from court by his half-brothers. These young men, sons of the slave that Charlot's mother, Berthe-aux-grands-pieds, substituted into King Pépin's marriage bed, poisoned Berthe and Pépin and relegated the legitimate heir Charlot to the kitchen. Charlot manages to escape with a group of followers, and he flees to the court of the Saracen king of Toledo, Galafre. Here, among his future sworn enemies, Charlot becomes a knight and a man.

The story of Charlemagne's youth began as a Latin text, the *Historia Karoli Magni et Rotholandi*, which is also known as the *Pseudo-Turpin Chronicle*.[19] Turpin, a contemporary of Charlemagne, was monk and treasurer at Saint-Denis. The author of the mid-twelfth century text takes on the guise of Turpin, and thus is known as Pseudo-Turpin. The Latin text tells the origins of the relics of Saint James of Compostella, relating how Charlemagne recovered them from the hands of the Saracens and established the shrine in Compostella. Compostella was the most popular pilgrimage site of medieval Europe, so establishing the history of the relics and their link to Charlemagne made popular reading. The Latin chronicle was soon translated into French and many other languages. While the Latin text is important in and of itself, the French texts are the focus of this study because they provide the link from myth to national consciousness. Since only the elite could read Latin, the stories that helped to create the notion of the nation of France were necessarily in the language of the people, French.

Forging Relationships: Law, "History," and National Identity 61

The French translations of the Pseudo-Turpin chronicle stretch throughout the thirteenth century. The story retells the *Chanson de Roland*, placing it in the context of the fictitious wars of Charlemagne against the Saracens. A text that borders on religious propaganda at times, it contains discussions between the Christians and the Muslims on the merits of the two religions. The adventures of the youthful Charles are referenced obliquely in a conversation between Charlemagne and the Saracen Agolant:

> Quant Agolanz oï Karles paller sarrazinois, si s'an mervoilla molt et s'an esjoï molt forment; et Karles l'avoit apris a paller a Tolote ou il demora grant piece quant il fu anfas.[20]

> [When Agolant heard Charles speak the Saracen language, he was much amazed and very happy about it. Charles had learned to speak it in Toledo, where he had stayed for a long time when he was a child.]

From this brief aside or the oral tradition behind it, one can surmise, the concept of the story of *Mainet* was born.

Curiously, in her study on foreign language-speaking in France in the twelfth and thirteenth centuries, Elisabeth Schulze-Busacker treats only one *chanson de geste*, the odd mixed-language *Girart de Roussillon*, and thus does not comment on Charlemagne's fictitious facility with language. Since this was the great period of the *chanson de geste*, this omission seems peculiar. Schulze-Busacker privileges Joinville's crusade account, which will be addressed in the next chapter, claiming that it illustrates "exceptional experiences and understanding of the Orient."[21] She finds Northern French literary production concerning foreigners and foreign languages to be "less open-minded and less interested in linguistic problems," theorizing that:

> Such minimal concern is certainly linked to the self-consciousness of the reinforced French kingdom at the end of the 12th century and continuing on into the 13th. French society (and literature) had acquired such a position of self-sufficiency on account of its predominance during the Crusades and in the world of chivalry, and of the economic power it exerted over tradesmen at the fairs in Champagne, that a glance abroad seemed of little importance.[22]

Such a view can only arise from a reading of the *chansons de geste* as pure fiction, meant solely to entertain, rather than the complex combination of historical account and pure invention that they actually embody. One need only consider the mid-twelfth century story of Mainet to see the centrality of the Other in defining the history of the France that Schulze-Busacker deems unconcerned about the foreigner.

The Old French Pseudo-Turpin translation illuminates Charles' childhood among the Saracens. Charles' collusion with the Saracen king of Toledo is explained by his ill-treatment at his stepbrothers' hands. A follower of Charles, Henri, proposes the move:

> Ains irons a Toulete en Espaigne la bele
> Au roi sarragouchan pour les armes conquerre
> A oes no petit roi, tant que puissons miels fere.²³
>
> [So, let's go to take up arms in Toledo in beautiful Spain, to the Saracen king, from what I hear not an insignificant king, so we can do better.]

Added to this burgeoning legend is the story of Charlemagne's wife Galienne, the Saracen daughter of the king of Toledo. According to the text, Charles and Galienne fall in love at the court of her father Galafre, king of Toledo. Galienne expresses her attraction to Charles:

> ... Car fust il ore voirs!
> Ja millor paradis ne querroie des mois,
> Le cors de moi et l'ame li metroie a son cois;
> Molt en seroie lie se en issoit uns oirs.²⁴
>
> [...That it should be true! Truly I have not been seeking a better paradise for a long time, I would put my body and soul at his liberty; I would be very happy if an heir should come of it.]

Galafre promises Galienne to Charles, but he is convinced by evil courtesans that he should allow his son, Marsile, to attack and kill Charles to stop the marriage. Galienne discovers the plot with the aid of her magic mirror:

> K'ele ert sage des ars et sot bien deviner
> Devers le ciel se torne pour le mirour garder.²⁵
>
> [For she was wise in the arts and knew how to tell the future. She turned toward the sky to look in the mirror.]

She alerts Charles to the danger:

> Mainet vauront ochire ains qu'il doie ajorner;
> Mais quant le sot Galie ne vaurra pas celer.²⁶
>
> [They wanted to kill Mainet as soon as daylight came, but when Galienne found out, hiding it will be no good.]

He defeats Marsile and marries the now-Christian Galienne. Upon his return to France, he defeats his half-brothers and takes up the crown as defender of the faith.

Like David and Christ, Charlemagne is the founder of a new, strong nation. His children will rule France after him. Placing a Saracen woman at the head of this lineage and as queen of France is a move that seems quite daring. Like Guillaume d'Orange's wife Guibourc, Galienne is successful in saving her future husband, and thus the French people, from the Saracens. The Saracen origin of the future queen of the French is not an exotic detail cooked up by the author, but rather an integral part of the founding of Charlemagne's new image. He comes from the very bosom of the enemy. Raised by them, speaking their language, understanding them, Charlemagne is able to conquer them.

Just as Bramimonde in the *Chanson de Roland* is converted "par amour," so Charlemagne tries to convert the pagans in the Pseudo-Turpin chronicles. He reasons with them and would have succeeded in turning Agolant to Christianity were it not for the bad example of some Christians. Alogant sees some poor people who are ill cared for by Christian society and cannot believe that the true God would allow his disciples to live in such deplorable conditions. Charlemagne, whose unique relationship with the Saracens would have allowed him to forge a union "par amour," must now fight the Infidel as the Biblical King David before him.

Nonetheless, this text celebrates the possibility of conversion, offered to the male Saracens and embodied in the acceptance of Galienne to convert and marry Charles. A new alliance between Christian and Saracen is possible if the Infidel will listen to reason. Unlike the *Chanson de Roland* and *Gormont et Isembart*, destruction is no longer the ultimate goal of the encounter with the Saracen. Ideally, conversion and integration would replace physical confrontation and death. The Infidel is seen to have a rational mind and a natural propensity toward truth. Were the Christians not their own worst ambassadors (Ganelon, those who mistreat the poor, the half-brothers of Charles), the Saracens might even be won over to the Christian camp. In the same way that Peter the Venerable encouraged understanding of the Saracen and his religion in order to better convert him, so the vernacular *chansons de geste* reveal openness to the Saracen Other that was not previously existent.

At least one contemporary European ruler, the Spaniard Alfonso VI of Toledo, embodied the ethic of Charlot. As A. de Mandach reports, Alfonso was often compared to Charlemagne. Sometimes referred to as Charlemagne and "Maynete" by contemporaries, Alfonso continued the connection with salvation history, representing the new Charlemagne, and thus the new Christ, who was the new David. In 1091 Alfonso VI married the Muslim princess Zaïda. The story of *Mainet* follows approximately the historical relationship and conflict between Alfonso and the brother of Zaïda, al-Mu'tamid. Needless to say, critics have found the tale of *Mainet* to be a timely justification for Alfonso's own personal history.[27] While *Mainet* postdates Alfonso's reign, twelfth century jurisprudence revolved around questions of marriage and legitimacy. So, the legitimacy of Alfonso's marriage was important both as his history was being written and for the prestige of his heirs. *Mainet* not only justifies, but celebrates, both his place in history and, even more so, the legitimacy of his heirs. For if Charlemagne could marry a pagan, then certainly Alfonso could not be reproached for doing likewise.

The link between nation and narration, between history and culture, is one that has been well theorized by post-colonial theorists. Frantz Fanon details the changes in the stories, the oral traditions, which take place as the literature of combat assumes a sense of responsibility. Literature becomes self-aware, realizing its role as expression of nationalism and national history. Fanon describes this movement:

> ...la littérature orale, les contes, les épopées, les chants populaires autrefois répertoriés et figés commencent à se transformer. Les conteurs que récitaient des épisodes inertes les animent et y introduisent de modifications de plus en plus fondamentales. Il y a tentative d'actualiser les conflits, de moderniser les formes de lutte évoquées, les noms des héros, le type des armes. La méthode allusive se fait de plus en plus fréquente. A la formule : "Il y a très longtemps de cela" on substitue celle plus ambiguï : "Ce qui va être rapporté s'est passé quelque part mais cela aurait pu se passer ici aujourd'hui ou demain."[28]

Halvdan Koht has located the expression of nationalism in twelfth-century Europe, and especially in the epic tale of the *Chanson de Roland*[29] As the story of Charlemagne and the Saracens evolves through the Pseudo-Turpin chronicles and *Mainet*, the sense of what happened long ago is replaced, as Fanon would suggest, with the conglomeration of Charlemagne with Alfonso VI. That is, more recent questions of Saracen and Christian interaction are merged with questions of nation formation. Destruction of the Saracen is no longer the ultimate goal, but conversion and integration.

What does it mean to link the history of your nation with that of your archenemy? It means that at least some writers were willing to see cooperation as a necessary part of the survival of their nation. If the Christian remained superior, he did so because of his relationship to truth. His job now was to spread that truth and incorporate members of non-believing societies. In defeating the Saracens from within, as the *sarrazinois*-speaking Charlemagne and Peter the Venerable advocate, Christian France emerges even stronger and more solidified than before. The gift of the Saracens, be it a magic mirror or the philosophy of Averroes, can be used by the Christians without fear to help make them wiser and invincible.

Exterminans, the beautiful and deadly two-faced portrait of the Infidel, appropriately demonstrates the mixed view of the twelfth- and thirteenth-century French author face-to-face with the Muslim. Attracted by the riches, luxury and philosophy that the proximity to the Saracen and the translation movement offered, the Western author exhibited a fascination with things Oriental (*sarrazinois*). Whereas previously a lack of knowledge about the Other led to an abstract longing and desire and a grudging admiration, now the Saracen represented extremes in both positive and negative qualities. The femininization of the positive Saracen qualities allowed the French to integrate into their society those elements of Muslim culture that they found attractive. Female, and yet powerful and wise, desired and desiring, lovely and yet foreign, the Saracen princess was so enigmatic that she could not pose a threat to the lines that French society was beginning to draw around itself. Even as Charlemage symbolized the formation of boundaries around the nascent French nation, the Saracen princess allowed the new community to incorporate other ideas and other peoples without sacrificing the continuity that was only starting to develop. While being undeniably Other in her strength, sensuality and magical powers, she was very French in her stylized beauty. With few changes, namely baptism, the Saracen could be incorporated into French life and even form the basis for a new dynasty, as in the case of Guibourc. The mixed community of Christians, Muslims and Jews could imagine a life together, with racial and national boundaries erased, if not religious ones. Not unsurprisingly, the boundaries between fiction, law and history showed an equal transparence. Just as the Usatges read like romance, so romance read as a legal treatise on marriage. This unproblematic view of cohabitation (ethnic and generic) was not to remain unchallenged. However, for a brief, magical period, access to the Other's world filled the imagination of many French authors, including those writing history and law.

NOTES

1. For an edition of Gratian in Old French, see Leena Löfstedt, Gratiani Decretum: la traduction en ancien français du Décret de Gratien, (Helsinki: Finnish Society of Sciences and Letters, 1992).
2. Jean Gaudemet, Le Mariage en Occident (Paris: Cerf, 1987), p. 148.
3. Kathryn Gravdal's Ravishing Maidens: writing rape in medieval French literature and law (Philadelphia : University of Pennsylvania Press, 1991) traces the continued interest in raptus through the High Middle Ages. For more information on rape in canon law, see in particular the work of James Brundage: "Carnal Delight: Canonistic Theories of Sexuality," in Proceedings of the Fifth International Congress of Medieval Canon, ed. Juttner and Pennington, Vatican City: Biblioteca Apostolica Vaticana, 1980: 361–85; "Rape and Marriage in the Medieval Canon Law," Revue de droit canonique 28 (1978): 62–75; "Rape and Seduction in the Medieval Canon Law," in Sexual Practices and the Medieval Church, ed. Bullough and Brundage, (Buffalo, NY: Prometheus Books, 1982), pp. 141–48; and Law, Sex, and Christian Society in Medieval Europe, (Chicago: University of Chicago Press, 1987).
4. The Usatges of Barcelona, trans. Donald J. Kagay, (Philadelphia: University of Pennsylvania Press, 1994), XI–3.
5. Siege de Barbastre, op. cit., lines 199–204.
6. Ibid., lines 2069–71.
7. Ibid., lines 5652–55.
8. Ibid., line 6095.
9. Ibid., lines 7167–68.
10. See in particular Augustine's Faith and Works, trans. Gregory J. Lombardo, (NY, NY: Newman Press, 1988), chapter 21.
11. Adhemar Esmein, Le mariage en droit canonique. Essays in history, economics and social science (New York: Burt Franklin, 1968), p. 216.
12. Siege de Barbastre, op. cit., lines 7247–49.

13. Esmein, op. cit., p. 29.
14. Ibid., p. 31.
15. *Siege de Barbastre*, op. cit., lines 7181–82.
16. Ibid., line 7264.
17. *Las Siete Partidas*, trans. Samuel Parsons Scott (Chicago: American Bar Association, 1931), section II.29.7.
18. Additional lines of the damaged manuscript are found in C. Samaran, "Lectures sous les rayons ultraviolets," *Romania* 53 (1927), pp. 291–97.
19. The Pseudo-Turpin exists in many different editions, including the following which were used for this study: Claude Buridant, ed. *La Traduction du Pseudo-Turpin du ms. Vatican Regina 624* (Geneva:Droz, 1976); Ronald N. Walpole, ed. *An Anonymous Old French Translation of the Pseudo-Turpin Chronicle* (Cambridge: Medieval Academy of America, 1979); Ronald N. Walpole, "The Burgundian Translation of the Pseudo-Turpin Chronicle in BN (French ms 25438)," *Romance Philology* 2 (1) (1948), pp. 177–215; Frederick Wulff, *La chronique dite Turpin* (Lund, 1881), and a Latin version, *Karolellus : atque Pseudo-Turpini Historia Karoli Magni et Rotholandi*, ed. Paul Gerhard Schmidt (Stuttgart: B.G. Teubneri, 1996).
20. Buridant, op. cit., p. 97.
21. Elisabeth Schulze-Busacker, "French Conceptions of Foreigners and Foreign Languages in the 12th and 13th Centuries," *Romance Philology* 41 (1987), p. 41.
22. Ibid., p. 41.
23. Buridant, op. cit., lines 93–95.
24. Ibid., lines 100–101.
25. Ibid., lines 85–86.
26. Ibid., lines 104–5.
27. A. de Mandach, *La Geste de Charlemagne et de Roland* (Geneva: Droz, 1961), p. 69.
28. Frantz Fanon, *Les damnés de la terre* (Paris: Gallimard, 1991), pp. 288–89.
29. Halvdan Koht, "The Dawn of Nationalism in Europe," *American Historical Review* 52 (1946–47), p. 266.

6. Questioning the Myth: Obstacle and Rejection

In 1241 the Mongol armies of the sons of Genghis Khan met and annihilated an army of German knights that tried to stop the Mongol invasion west of the river Oder. While Western Europeans had managed to turn a blind eye as the Mongols conquered China, Persia, Russia, and parts of Hungary and Poland, the threat of the Mongols now reached their own backyards. With such imminent danger, the concerns of the West might be expected to turn from the Saracen to the Mongol. This was not immediately the case, however. First, having been convinced that the Khan was in fact the legendary Prester John, a powerful Christian ruler in Asian lands, the Pope and St. Louis decided to try to convince the Mongols to ally with them to defeat the Saracens. The Khan, who had to this point experienced no troubles in overrunning a large part of Europe and Asia, was understandably uninterested in St. Louis' proposal. In 1260, the Mongols pushed their way to Jerusalem, where the Mamluks held firm and dealt them a first, yet definitive, defeat.

At the same time as these invasions, Ramon Llull, the Catalan poet turned missionary, began preaching the need to convert the Arabs, Turks, and Mongols who surrounded the Christian empire. Unlike previous unsuccessful attempts that focused mainly on conversion by the sword, Llull proposed that missionaries learn the languages, customs, and cultures of the lands of the Infidel to preach more effectively the Gospel. The missions inspired and led by Llull met with no better success than the Crusades had. Not only was there resistance on the part of Christian religious leaders to study Islam and Arabic, but also the Muslims perceived the strong-arm preaching of Llull and his followers as arrogance and blasphemy, resulting in even greater conflict and misunderstanding. As a final blow to the hopes of the missionaries, in 1295 the Mongol chief Gazan converted to Islam, as Llull had both predicted and greatly feared.

The death of Llull made a decisive blow to hope for interaction between East and West. Little wonder that the West finally gave up plans to overtake the Orient, either by force or by reason. Disillusionment had been a long time in the making, however. Thoughts of assimilation and integration, as revealed in *chansons de geste* like *Prise d'Orange* and embodied in the literary persona of the amorous Saracen princess, began to seem less and less likely and appealing. Starting in the late twelfth century, more stories began to be told which focused on the obstacles of integration, rather than the possibilities. Rejection of the Saracen as ignoble or savage, certainly far from the courtly depictions of the Saracen armies in the *Chanson de Roland*, replaced awe and marvel in certain literary images of the Orient and its peoples.

An example of this shift in perception is found in tracing the romance epic, a genre that began in the twelfth century and continued until the end of the French Middle Ages, into the fifteenth century. One of the earliest romance epics is the mid-twelfth-century *Floire et Blancheflor*.[1] The story of a captive Christian woman who marries a Muslim ruler, after converting him and his people, finds its inverse in the story of *Aucassin et Nicolette*. Following the model of Blancheflor, the early thirteenth century Nicolette, a captured Muslim woman in Christian lands, converts and marries a Christian count. The theme of capture and intermarriage continues with the *Fille du comte de Ponthieu*, a thirteenth-century tale of an already-married Christian woman who finds herself captive in Muslim lands and converts to Islam to marry the Sultan, only to desert him later and return to her Christian husband. By the fourteenth century, the Christian Alis in *Lion de Bourges* (barely) avoids intermarriage by masquerading as a man when Muslims capture her. A later version of the *Fille du comte de Ponthieu* shows how the fifteenth-century audience reread the earlier story and altered it to fit later sensibilities.

These stories all share two common elements: movement between cultures and the exchange of women. Over time, changing cultures becomes more difficult and complex, just as the exchange of women becomes less and less voluntary and is finally completely rejected. The space of the Orient becomes an arena for the playing-out of the interethnic fantasy, providing simultaneously an element of desire and danger. Examining the trip to the Orient in each of these romances exposes the historical and perceptional change in relationship between East and West.

Along with physical differences, one of the clear problems for envisioning interaction with Saracens was that of reaching the domain of the Other. Travel was not uncommon in medieval Europe, and pilgrimages and crusade led medieval Europeans to Muslim lands, but literary representations of the voyage to the Orient are not simplistic. The earliest epics, *La Chanson de Roland*, *La Chanson de Guillaume* and *Gormont et Isembart*, did not involve travel into Saracen country. The Saracens were met and defeated in the open, on Christian lands. These were lands that had been temporarily held by the Saracen but were nonetheless essentially Christian. The twelfth-century literary voyage, unlike the early epics, finally took the Christian into the stronghold of the Saracen, into the magical castles in Spain that the

Saracens occupied. One could not simply walk or ride on horseback to a Saracen castle. The trip took on the topos of the "aventure merveilleuse." To say "getting there was half the fun" is no exaggeration in describing the roundabout ways that the French voyager entered the domains of his or her Saracen counterpart.

The beginning of the *Siege de Barbastre* is like the older epics. A blood-covered messenger comes from Saracen territories where he has been held captive to announce the imminent arrival of the Infidel. The Saracens soon swarm over the French, who are holed up at Narbonne. In a battle at the foot of the Narbonnais fortress, Bueves and companions are taken prisoner and sent to the Saracen stronghold at Barbastre. The donjon at Barbastre, a marvel of Roman engineering, is described:

> Rois Julius Cesaires la fist par amistés.
> Tous li pires carrel est a cissel ovrés,
> A metal ou a plom bien assis et fondés.[2]
>
> [King Julius Caesar made it as a sign of friendship. It is square, all the stones wrought by chisel, well set and fixed in metal or lead.]

In this impregnable tower, the French are being held, but with the help of a Saracen turncoat, the French capture the tower from within. At that point, the Amirant, leader of the Saracens, is notified and leaves his siege at Narbonne to come and besiege the small French company holding Barbastre. The Saracen who leaves the fortress at Barbastre to bring the Amirant the news must slip out, and his route betrays at once a lack of interest in veritable geography along with a fascination for the exotic:

> Corsolt de Tabarie est de Barbastre enblés
> Sor .i. blanc dromadaire qui n'estoit pas lassés.
> Passe Rune et Serine, les pors de Balegués,
> Et costoie Leride et Cordres de delés,
> Et est venus a Aude, dont parfont est li gués.[3]
>
> [Corsolt de Tabarie galloped out of Barbastro on a white camel that was not tired. He passed the Rhône and the Serein, and the gates of Balaguer, and he skirted the side of Lerida and Cordoba quickly, and he came to Aude, where the ford is deep.]

This trip to the Orient is extremely suspect. The trip takes place incredibly quickly, considering that Corsolt is undertaking it on a camel. Then, in leaving from Barbastro in Spain, he passes by the Rhône (far in the wrong direction) in order to arrive at Aude.

Likewise, when Malatrie is called up to join her father at Barbastre, the trip undertaken is a fantastic one. She mounts in a ship so richly appointed that "La barge au roi Judas n'i valsist .i. denier"[4] [King Judas' ship wasn't worth a *denier* next to it]. Along with a special bread kitchen and a wine cellar, the ship is equipped with a "mahomerie" (as the French liked to term the imaginary location where the Muslims worshipped idols) and a windmill. Finally, when Girart slips out of Barbastre to call for reinforcements, he does so by the "porte turcoise" as Raymond Weeks appropriately calls it,⁵ a secret subterranean passage,⁶ another indication that the passage between Christian and Muslim lands must be accomplished with the help of magic or engineering marvels.

In *La Prise d'Orange*, Guillaume penetrates the central tower where Orable, the wife of his Saracen archenemy, is closeted. Philip Bennett has termed his ingression as a "storming of the Other World," linked to the already common theme of the Conquest of the Land of the Dead.⁷ The story of the taking of Orange has evolved, Bennett notes, to surpass this preexistent theme of entrance into a surreal, deadly landscape. All paths into Orange involve complicated crossings of water. In addition, the stronghold, an imposing marble tower named Gloriete in the center of Orange, is virtually impenetrable and completely indestructible. The only person who knows its secret tunnel-entrances is Orable herself.

This voyage is one of sexual initiation for the French crusaders. Desire is clear in the set up of the tower, both desire for Orable sexually (she and her surroundings are described as most opulent and sensual) as well as desire for the power which possession of Orable will produce. The link between the town and the woman is made concrete, as the author pens: "Ja ne quier mes lance n'escu porter/Se ge nen ai la dame et la cite."⁸

Grosrichard, who writes on the seraglio in eighteenth-century literature, notes that the image of the seraglio is stereotyped and does not change from one literary work to the next. He theorizes:

> . . . on se répète, on se copie (tout en prétendant chaque fois qu'on apporte de nouveau, de l'inédit), parce que l'image stéréotypée du sérail, composée au début du XVIIe siècle, répond sans doute exactement à ce qu'on en attend.⁹

If the reader had a certain image in mind, this image began to be created not in the seventeenth century, but as far back as the twelfth century. The location of the power of the oriental ruler, like his early modern counterpart, was in the heart of the seraglio itself. The tower of Orange, center of passion and also heart of the city of Orange, shows this duality long before the seventeenth century.

Like the stereotyped seraglio of later centuries, the Saracen stronghold is always the same. The *Siege de Barbastre* includes several speeches by French soldiers who recall the circumstances of other sieges where Bueves came to help his lord or relative. The messengers remind those who owe Bueves a debt for helping to free them so that they will, in turn, come to his rescue in Barbastre. These sieges foreshadow the sieges of Barbastre and Orange. Of all places, in the impregnable tower where the French are imprisoned with mighty Saracen forces surrounding them, the French and the Saracen lovers are to meet and exchange promises. This common theme, the Saracen princess aiding the French warrior, repeats itself over and over in French *chansons de geste* and Latin tales. Like an outsider who has slipped into the deadly seraglio, the French soldier has managed to encounter the Saracen woman on her own turf, in the very place where she holds sway. Like the phallic women, the women with power over men that Grosrichard locates in the seraglio,[10] the Saracen princess is the true master of this interior space of the *donjon*.

The fantastic geography of travel to the Orient illustrates the just one of many obstacles that were raised between Christian and Muslim interaction. Literary sources spoke in these terms, allegorical terms, to refer to the differences in religion and culture that prohibited or discouraged intermixing. By examining fictional travel accounts in light of their allegorical nature, perceptions of Christian-Saracen interaction take on new light.

Often considered to be a parody of *Floire et Blancheflor*,[11] *Aucassin et Nicolette* clearly owes much to its predecessor.[12] The two stories are largely inversions of each other. Floire, the Arab with a Christian-inspired name, falls in love with Blancheflor, the daughter of a Christian slave. Floire's unfeeling father intentionally separates the lovers because their marriage would be socially inappropriate. Yet Floire, through his persistence, manages to reunite the couple. Nicolette, the Arab slave with a Christian name, and Aucassin, the Christian noble with a Saracen-sounding name, likewise conceive an inappropriate love and are separated by disapproving fathers. Through her ingenuity and everlasting love, Nicolette enables the couple to marry.

The stories share many elements of the standard Oriental fantasy that was found in the *chansons de geste* and lyric poetry. Among the more salient of these characteristics was the alternance of reality and myth in geographical representation of the Orient. While a great deal of knowledge was available in the eleventh and twelfth centuries about Andalusia and the Holy Land, authors usually inserted an element of the fantastic when describing the Orient. In looking at the ways that *Aucassin et Nicolette* and *Floire et Blancheflor* both echo the standard geographic model of the Orient and diverge from it (and, more importantly, each other), the parodic element of *Aucassin et Nicolette* seems nostalgic of an earlier period, where as in *Floire et Blancheflor* hope for mastery of the Orient still reigned. The movement from desire for integration to isolationism becomes evident.

In the standard medieval romance plot, a boat bound for Christian lands is whisked off-course by a violent, unexpected storm. When the clouds lift, the passengers discover to their dismay that they have been transported to the Orient, to Saracen lands. After a period of adaptation and integration in the pagan country, the stranded Christian travelers find their way back to France where they are welcomed with great honor and increased social status.

Variations of this theme permeate the romance literature of the French Middle Ages. The space of the Orient has rightfully been labeled "un espace ludique, un divertissement, une fuite hors du réel."[13] The marvels of the East as they were laid bare to crusaders and pilgrims of the eleventh and twelfth centuries provided ideal fodder for the imagination of medieval writers. Extraordinary fabrics, spices, scents and architecture piqued the senses of the western traveler. The science and philosophy of the East impressed occidental literati. Yet the Orient was also a land that was essentially unknown. Vast regions of even the Near East remained uncharted for Europeans for centuries to come. Within these unknown spaces, literary invention and imagination had free reign, creating lands of incredible richness and monstrous delights. Within this context of Oriental fantasy, E. Faral's contention appears justified:"Qu'il s'agisse des voyages merveilleux . . . ou de cet Orient fabuleux qui a communiqué ses couleurs à tant de récits, ou du burlesque des contes à rire et des fabliaux, ce ne sont partout que rêves, fantaisies et jeux."[14]

However, the Orient was not simply or uniquely an imaginary space. While early geography, which placed Gog and Magog along with the Tower of Babel on a physical map, seems fantastic to modern sensibility, for the cartographers of the early centuries of this millennium the Orient, along with its marvels, was indeed a physical space with real characteristics. The Orient was not only fantasy but also reality.[15] Trading relations, pilgrimage routes and crusades made the Orient a space of encounter as well as imagination. Thus the literary voyage to the Orient should be read within this complex duality of myth and reality, taking into account the implications of multi-layered meaning for a single location on a medieval map.

Views of the medieval world are available in both verbal and pictorial accounts. In the twelfth century, when the genre of romance was born and flourished in France, the world was often seen as a round disk, surrounded by water and divided into three parts, Europe, Africa and Asia, by the T-shaped intersection of the seas separating the regions.[16] Danielle Lecoq and J.-P. Magnier have reconstructed the stereotypical map of the second quarter of the twelfth century, further dividing the East into Babylonia and Egypt (figure 1). The Lecoq-Magnier sketch indicates the placement of Carthage, Rome and Troy, three of the cities which were most frequented in the medieval literary voyage. The map is oriented with the extreme East (Oriens) at the top and the West (Occidens) at the bottom. In the center is the Holy Land. At the top of the map is located the Earthly Paradise from which Adam and Eve were expelled. A scene of the Last Judgment wraps around the lower half of the map, as the sword-wielding angel sends some to the maws of Hell and others to the warm embrace of the Heavenly Host.

Heaven and Hell occupy liminal spaces in the geography of the world, neither being on the map nor off the map. Their physical location was uncertain and formed the basis of a great range of opinion by medieval thinkers. However, the Earthly Paradise, or the Garden of Eden, was often believed to be a real spot, perhaps on an island, in the Far Eastern regions of the world. The Earthly Paradise necessarily occupied a relatively unknown region, since no medieval person had ever visited it, so the Orient was a logical choice for its location. Perhaps more importantly, the Orient at the same time furnished a spiritual reading for the position of Eden. Closer to God, at the top of the world, Eden cradled man in his time of innocence.

The verbal map of Hugh of Saint-Victor indicates both the spiritual and the physical dimensions of the medieval *mappemonde*. The most illustrious teacher at what would become the school of Saint-Victor in Paris, Hugh made an enormous impact on thought in the early twelfth century. Termed the "new Augustine," Hugh died in Saint-Victor in 1141. His ideas on the geography of the world, expounded in a small treatise called "De Arca Noe Mystica," form a logical backdrop for the study of geography in middle twelfth-century French romance. For that reason, his verbal map is worth quoting in full:

> Divine Providence, making it so that the events that at the beginning of time took place in the East were located in a way at the beginning of space while the center of things then moved toward the West as time ran its course, wanted to bring us to understand that the end of our era is near because the passage of history has already reached the end of space.

> The first man was placed in the East from his creation and from this original point his descendants must cover the Earth. Likewise, after the flood, it was in the East that empires were born; it was the center of the world for the Assyrians, the Chaldeans, and the Medeans. Then the center moved toward Greece, before supreme power then descended near the end of time to the West, to the Romans, who live in a way at the end of the world. Thus, while the movement of major events moved down in a straight line from east to west, that which took place on the right and on the left, that is to say in the directions of the Aquila and the Auster, corresponds to meanings so precise that all men who think seriously about it cannot deny that things were made that way following the Divine Plan. In a few words, in relationship to Jerusalem, Egypt is at the south and Babylon is at the north. Egypt means "shadows" and the wind from the south is hot. Egypt designates thus this world, plunged in the shadows of ignorance and the heat of carnal desire. Babylon means "confusion" and signifies the hell where disorder and eternal cold reign.[17]

The very real locations on the medieval map embodied corresponding vices and virtues. While the East lay closer to God and His Grace, the original sin began the inexorable movement of world dominance from East to West. Spiritual enlightenment had moved toward the West, but also from North to South. Babylon, which once knew the Truth, was plunged into confusion. Egypt had not yet been converted, remaining in ignorance and sin. The disposition of the world map gives to each location both a physical and a spiritual meaning. The movement of time, from Eden to the Last Judgment, coincides with the movement of God's grace.

Geography and meaning were inseparably intertwined. The medieval romance writer used this multi-layered geography to add to the meaning of his or her story. Action that takes place in the East cannot be read as merely another episode.[18] Nor can the marvels of the East be reduced to a desire for opulence and color in a story, as Philippe Sénac's characterization would have us believe:

> Surtout, l'Islam devient synonyme d'exotisme, de luxe de raffinement. L'embellissement est de règle . . . L'Orient devient un univers de splendeurs et d'objets rares.[19]

Since the voyage to the East poses a problem to the modern reader, many studies have opted not to account for these trips,[20] or treat them as trivial or proclaim them straightforward parody.[21] The voyage to the Orient, however, illustrates how a medieval author makes use of geographical and imaginary space in medieval French romance to give the *roman* a nuanced meaning.

The trip to the Orient is geographically detailed in the mid twelfth-century *Floire et Blancheflor*. Blancheflor is sold to the Emir of Babiloine by merchants, who had in turn bought this daughter of a Christian slave from Floire's father, the Saracen king of Naples, Spain. J.-L. Leclanche identifies the kingdom of Floire's father as Niebla, which was in the twelfth century the capital of a small Muslim monarchy.[22] Since the story clearly indicates that the king is "paiiens"[23] and from Spain, this logical conclusion explains the rejection of any connection with Naples, Italy. Likewise, Leclanche indicates the probable locations for several other cities. Montoire, where Floire is sent to study, is logically linked to Montoro, in Andalusia.[24] However, when the author describes the trip to the Orient, to Babiloine, Leclanche opines that this previously geographically astute author is now guilty of "flou géographique."[25] The Babiloine of the *roman* becomes Cairo, which was also often known as Babylone in the Middle Ages. With this determination, a chain of geographical mistakes by the author of the roman results. Clearly, one does not pass by Badaus,[26] which is Baghdad, to get to Cairo, so Baghdad must then be Alexandria for Leclanche.[27] The river Enfer,[28] which must be crossed for Floire to enter Babiloine, cannot then be El Fern, the Arabic name for the Syrian Oronte. Leclanche determines that this must be a branch of the Nile, since the story must take place in Egypt.

Accusations of geographic fluidity do not fully describe the mapping of *Floire et Blancheflor*. Linguistically, the author is first of all describing Babiloine as a place, rather than as a city. Whereas movement toward other cities uses the expected preposition "a," as in "a Naples,"[29] "a Montoire,"[30] and "a Baudas,"[31] for Babiloine the country prefix "en" is used, as in "en Babiloine."[32] "Babiloine la cité"[33] indicates the main city, where the Emir lives and where the action will take place. El Fern and Baghdad are both locations in the Babylone of twelfth-century cartographers. The First Crusade of 1096-1099 brought French crusaders through Syria and not far from Baghdad itself. Stories involving the crusaders' route had doubtless reached the West in the sixty years before the text was written. The author of the text is still geographically incorrect. Baghdad is not a port town and so Floire could not have actually sailed into the city. However, unlike Alexandria, which was well known to the medieval West and so would hardly be misnamed, Baghdad is in the third of the world named Babylone by cartographers. Additionally, Baghdad was the center of Islam until 1171 when Saladin moved the center of the empire to Egypt. Since the Babiloine of this text from circa 1150 contrasts so sharply with Western Christian ideas of marriage and paradise, the author probably means to critique the entire Muslim society. The center of interest would then lie in Baghdad and not yet in Cairo.

The importance in reading Babiloine as a region is that the author has placed the action of the text in that mystical and yet real region of the world where the Earthly Paradise was located. Babylone, as can be seen from the map of Henri de Mayence (figure 2), would include the land of the Tower of Babel as well as Gog and Magog. Across Babylone, the Earthly Paradise lay as a locale that was at once theoretically reachable and yet in practice unattainable to the medieval traveler.

The city of Babiloine in the text mirrors this mythical location. The remarkable garden enclosed within its walls titillates the senses of sight and smell and serves as the sexual proving ground of the girls the Emir wishes to wed. If their virginity has been lost, water ripples, speaking out against them. The Euphrates, considered at that time to be one of the four rivers of Paradise, is named "uns flueves de paradis"[34] and runs along one side of the garden. The garden is directly linked to the Earthly Paradise by the author, who writes:

> Qui ens est et sent les odors
> et des espisses et des flors
> et des oisiaus oïst les sons
> et haus et bas les gresillons,
> por la douçor li est avis
> des sons qu'il est en paradis.[35]
>
> [Whoever is inside and smells the fragrances and the spices and the flowers and hears the sounds of the birds, and the high and low chirping, due to the sweetness of the sounds he is convinced that he is in paradise.]

When Floire begins his journey, he realizes that he is en route to his own Earthly Paradise, where Blancheflor lives. He eagerly and generously pays his passage on a merchant ship:

> car vis li est k'en paradis
> l'a mis quant il est el païs
> u s'amie cuide trover
> que il siut par terre et par mer.[36]

[for he is of the opinion that he has been put in paradise when he is in the country where he thinks to find his love, whom he follows by land and by sea]

This paradise, as exquisite as it may seem, can never be the real Earthly Paradise. Thinkers from Isidore of Seville to Peter Comestor took pains to point out that man could not attain the Earthly Paradise.[37] The thirteenth-century *Voyage d'Alexandre au Paradis terrestre* denies even the great Alexander the possibility of entering the walls of the Earthly Paradise, located near the Ganges. The *roman* of *Floire et Blancheflor* is set in precisely the same location as Alexander's voyages. Not incidently, the name of Floire's host in Babiloine, Daries, evokes the Dayres of the *Roman d'Alexandre*, the ruler of Persia and India who was defeated by Alexander. The location of the Earthly Paradise, as set down in the earliest Alexander romances, coincides with Babiloine and its perverse garden.

Babiloine is one of those non-Paradise paradises that were so popular in medieval literature. While elements of the true Paradise can be found at the site, a necessary warping has taken place. This corrupted paradise is really no paradise at all, for the girls who marry the pagan Emir are condemned to die. The opposite of the Garden of Eden, Babiloine is the center of hopelessness and eternal death for those belong to the Emir. Just as Hugh of Saint-Victor had defined Babylone as that which "veut dire 'confusion' et signifie l'enfer où règnent le désordre et le froid éternel," so the Babiloine of the roman is a muddled Eden which is more aptly termed "Hell."

In *Aucassin et Nicolette* the trip to the geographical Orient is replaced by a voyage to a spiritual Orient, Muslim Spain. If the medieval writer used Andalusia as substitute for the Orient, little changed in the representation of the locale. Because of the cultural links between the Muslim worlds of the East and West, the similarity in treatment is not only allegorical in nature but practical as well. Based on shared literary language and some religious traditions, the geographical Far East and Far West on the medieval map could be imagined as almost identical locations. As Hugh's allegorical reading of the world would show, God's grace had not yet reached the extreme end of the Occident.

Though a trip to the Orient forms an integral part of the story, the equivalent of Babiloine in *Aucassin et Nicolette* is not the Spanish Muslim city of Cartage where Nicolette finds her roots, but rather the uncharted magical land of Torelore. Sexuality is perverted in this land, as in Babiloine, as the king gives birth while his wife is leading the troops. Just as Floire's journey leads to the end of the Emir's cruel execution of his wives, so Aucassin beats the king until he agrees that "ja mais hom en vo tere d'enfant ne gerra" [never will any man in your land give birth to a child].[38]

The theme of the upside-down world, the perverse paradise, is perhaps the most salient feature of *Aucassin et Nicolette* and is echoed in Aucassin's infamous "Heaven and Hell" speech. Nonetheless, the author opts not to locate Torelore in the East. The implications of this choice in the parodic text of *Aucassin et Nicolette* are intriguing. Since the author plays quite openly with the standard travel-adventure tale, especially *Floire et Blancheflor*, he or she could be indicating that the old model of the East as land of confusion is outdated or trite. María Rosa Menocal has suggested that the story has a pluralistic, "why can't we all just get along?" ring to it, which would certainly justify the positioning of a topsy-turvy world in the West where it would normally be found in the East.[39] By showing that the Occident can contain the same anti-paradise as the Orient, the author accuses the West of the same confusion that had often been equated with the East.

Many elements of Torelore do in fact seem paradisiacal. The wars are really food fights, and the inhabitants of Torelore are appalled when Aucassin actually kills some of their enemies. Nonetheless, Torelore is a land of leisure, and in medieval literature, such a place is only a deceptive paradise. Just as Chrétien de Troyes' Erec is reproached for his "recreantise" with Enide, so the capture of Aucassin and Nicolette occurs because they have been so enjoying their dalliances in the magical land that they do not protect themselves from a Saracen raid. As Floire cannot remain in the Emir's tower forever enjoying the love of Blancheflor, so Aucassin et Nicolette are not allowed to neglect their responsibilities to the outside world, the real world, the Christian world. The stay in the perverse paradise must come to an end.

One does not simply travel to and from the Orient at will in twelfth-century medieval romance. Either the Orient draws the visitor unwillingly to its shores, or one crosses stealthily over its borders. Contrary to the typical romance models, medieval and Renaissance travelers would eagerly seek out the Earthly Paradise. The romance traveler was literally often dragged to the Orient. As with Nicolette, who just happens upon her hometown, and Floire, who stays at the same inn as his beloved sosie Blancheflor, the Orient draws to it those who need to visit its lands.

Nicolette and Aucassin enjoy their leisure in Torelore until Saracen merchants attack the indolent country, taking the two lovers captive and whisking them away in different ships. The force of Nature collaborates with the separation of the lovers that will eventually lead to their permanent reconciliation in Provence:

> si leva une tormente par mer que les espartist. Li nés u Aucassins estoit ala tant par mer waucrant qu'ele ariva au castel de Biaucaire[40]...La nés u Nicolete estoit estoit le roi de Cartage[41] . . . Il nagierent tant qu'il ariverent desox le cité de Cartage, et quant Nicolete vit les murs del castel et le païs, ele se reconut . . .[42]

> [A storm rose up on the sea that separated them. The ship where Aucassin was wandered so much in the ocean that it arrived at the castle of Biaucaire. The ship Nicolette was on belonged to the king of Carthage. It

sailed such that it arrived beneath the city of Carthage, and when Nicolette saw the walls of the city and the country, she recognized herself.]

A mythical force almost divinely guided, the storm that separates the idle lovers of Torelore reminds them of their responsibilities toward society. Aucassin must take over the rule of his father's lands. Nicolette must understand that she is not a lower-class pagan slave, but a princess worthy of a great marriage. She must fully reject her Saracen past, saying to herself:

> Tant mar fui de haut parage,
> ne fille au roi de Cartage,
> ne cousine l'amuaffle!
> Ci me mainnent gent sauvages.[43]

> [Little good it did me to be well born, the daughter of the king of Carthage, and the cousin of the emir! Those who have me are a savage people.]

As an insider, her rejection of the Saracens as uncultured carries an even greater weight. The final scene as she removes the black color from her face represents a definitive rejection of her other life. Through her movement back in time, to her childhood past via the twelfth-century equivalent of the resurrection of "hidden memories," she may integrate herself with the French present.

The borders between the Orient and the Occident are not permeable to the naive traveler. Only certain classes appear able to travel between the East and West without harm, namely merchants and male entertainers. When Nicolette wishes to return to the West, she must disguise herself, blackening her face with an herb and wearing the clothes of a male bard, in order to sneak passage on a merchant ship.

Floire, knowing that he cannot search for Blancheflor as the son of a king, explains to his father that he will disguise himself, "comme marceans le querrai"[44] [as a merchant I will look for her]. No one seems particularly impressed by his disguise, either. Both of his hosts on the trip immediately recognize that he is not of the merchant class; he is much too refined and obviously in love. One of his hosts, Daries, proposes that he masquerade as an architect to gain entrance into the tower where Blancheflor is held.

The trip that is made between East and West is a spiritual journey, a quest that must change the relationship between the traveler himself/herself and the outside world. Eugene Vance argues that the traveler remains a one-dimensional character:

> As is the case with so much medieval narrative, the plot of Aucassin et Nicolette is constructed upon the fixed nature of its characters, and a change of heart in any major character would cause the whole tale to collapse.[45]

However, at least one character in the romances under study changes drastically due to his or her trip to the East. As a direct result of the voyage that proves his right to marry Blancheflor, Floire is converted from Islam to Christianity. Aucassin evolves due to his separation from Nicolette; he must rule Biaucaire, and he does so with strength of resolve that he did not exhibit even at the end of their adventure in Torelore. Nicolette fully understands her past and can thus finally reject it.

W. Kibler has also noticed the essential change in the traveller, claiming: "this voyage of the hero to an 'Otherworld' is a classical archetypal expression of the individuation process."[46] If individuation results from these trips, social integration appears to be the more salient result of the voyage. Whereas the couples of Floire and Blacheflor and Aucassin and Nicolette would not have been able to rule their lands before owing to their anti-social love affairs, both couples are acclaimed as rulers of strength and unity in their lands after contact with the Orient.

Yet if the voyage to the East contains the story of an individual's self development, it also necessarily tells the tale of contact between two cultures. Such juxtaposition, voluntary or involuntary, leads to an inevitable change in not only the individual, but also the relationships between the two nations.

The journey that Floire makes to the anti-heaven of Babiloine is a movement in Time that coincides with Hugh's verbal *mappamundi*. As Time is moving from East to West, movement to the East implies a movement back in Time. This Time coincides with religious or spiritual Time, the period of God's grace and the focus of God's interest as it evolves from the Garden of Eden down through the Greeks and to the West. The story of *Floire et Blancheflor* is in fact the history of the conversion of Hungary, a vital moment in tenth century Christian politics. The story opens with the essential outcome of the tale:

> Puis que Flores fu crestiiens,
> li avint grans honors et biens,
> car puis fu rois de Hongerie
> et de trestoute Bougerie.[47]

> [Since Floire was (became) a Christian, great honor and wealth came to him. He became king of Hungary and of almost all of Bulgaria.]

Floire's history is necessarily a movement back to pagan time, before God's grace had reached Hungary. Floire's obligatory return to the West, from Babiloine to Hungary, illustrates the inexorable march of God's grace westward. The Christian must understand that which came before, that which was once Paradise but then became corrupted, to better see the spiritual vision of the West. *Floire et Blancheflor* helps explain that evolution.

Jean Favier contends that the conversion of the Hungarians led to new safety on the pilgrimage route to the Holy Land for Christians.[48] The pilgrimage, central to twelfth century spiritual life, figures prominently in the *roman*. The Emir captures Blancheflor's mother as she and Blancheflor's father make a pilgrimage to Compostella. Balancing the opening ill-fated pilgrimage, the story closes on the conversion of Floire and his baptism of his people. Those who refuse baptism are burnt alive or decapitated. Through the daughter who causes the conversion of an entire country, a new, safer pilgrimage route is established. Likewise, Nicolette, once considered unacceptable as a spouse for the noble Aucassin, integrates into French society and will be the mother of future heirs.

But these seemingly similar stories of integration and cultural interaction hide an important difference. Whereas in *Floire et Blancheflor* the entire community of Niebla and Hungary is converted to Christianity because of the exemplary love of the two young lovers, in *Aucassin et Nicolette* the focus is on rejection of Islam and the Arab culture rather than on the conversion and continued positive interaction of two different peoples. Even Babiloine is made almost acceptable to Christian morals, and the sense is certainly made clear that both Floire and Blancheflor would be welcome back to the now-happy kingdom. The text ends on an upbeat note, with open possibilities about future happy exchanges and perhaps even the eventual conversion of that anti-paradise, Babiloine. *Aucassin et Nicolette* offers no such solace. Nicolette had been baptized long before she even undertook her journey home. As she rejects her people, Nicolette eliminates the eventuality of further exchange. The door is shut between the peoples of Carthage and Biaucaire. The fantastic voyage that allowed a momentary sharing of ideas is a trip not to be repeated.

Travel to the Orient constitutes a theme in medieval literature that can for all practical purposes be considered a genre in itself. What began as a way for the French to access and conquer the Saracens was fairly straightforward in the *Chanson de Roland*; travel and geography were basically believable and verifiable. Romance epic, with its trick entrances into fantastic castles lorded over by Saracen women, introduced a magical element to the genre. For *Aucassin et Nicolette* and *Floire et Blanchflor*, the trip itself becomes the story. The travel romance continues to hold sway in French literature on into the fifteenth century (and beyond), precisely because of its possibility for juxtaposing two different cultures.

NOTES

1. For the dating of *Floire et Blanchflor*, M. Delbouille proposed 1160–61, claiming intertextuality with *Brut*, *Roman de Thebes* and *Enéas* ("A propos de la patrie et de la date de Floire et Blancheflor," *Mélanges Mario Roques*, IV, Paris, 1952). Leclanche favors a date before the separation of Louis VII and Eleanor of Aquitaine in 1152 (*Romania* 92, p. 566). I. Cluzel and M. de Riquier have offered further evidence for the date of 1150. For a complete overview of the dating debate, see J.-L. Leclanche, *Contribution á l'Ètude de la transmission des plus anciennes oeuvres romanesques françaises. Un cas privilégié: Floire et Blancheflor*. Thesis Paris-Sorbonne (Lille, 1980).

2. Raymond Weeks, "The Siège de Barbastre," *Romanic Review* 10 (4) (1919), p. 304.
3. Ibid., p. 306.
4. Ibid., p. 309.
5. Ibid., p. 321.
6. *Le Siege de Barbastre*, ed. J.L. Perrier (Paris: Champion, 1926), line 3263.
7. Philip Bennett, "The Storming of the Other World, the Enamoured Muslim Princess, and the Evolution of the Legend of Guillaume d'Orange," *Guillaume d'Orange and the Chanson de Geste*, ed. Wolfgang Emden (Reading: Société Rencesvals, 1984), p. 3.
8. Ibid., p. 5.
9. Alain Grosrichard, *Structure du sérail: la fiction du despotisme asiatique dans l'Occident classique* (Paris: Éditions du Seuil, 1979), p. 155.
10. Ibid., p. 208.
11. Articles espousing and exposing the parodic element of the text include the study by Mariantonia Liborio, Italian translator of the text, Jean Dufournet's critical edition, and two articles each by Eugene Vance and Tony Hunt. The parodic view of the text has been challenged, to my view unsuccessfully, by Joseph Garreau, but his article remains useful for its summary of previous scholarship. See bibliography for references to these articles.
12. Citations from the following editions of these texts: *Aucassin et Nicolette*, ed. Mario Roques (Paris: Champion, 1973); *Floire et Blancheflor*, ed. J.-L. Leclanche (Paris: Champion, 1983).
13. Philippe Sénac, *L'image de l'autre: histoire de l'occident médiéval face à Islam*, (Paris: Flammarion, 1983), p. 86.
14. Edmond Faral, "Introduction," *Dictionnaire des lettres françaises: le Moyen Age*, ed. Bossuat et. al. (Paris: Fayard, 1992), p. XXI.
15. For an excellent study on the real and fantastic elements in medieval geography, see Chantal Connochie-Bourgne, "L'Orient, réalité et discours, dans l'Image du Monde," *Images et Signes de L'Orient dans l'Occident Médiéval*, ed. Arrouye, Aix-en-Provence: Université de Provence, 1982.
16. Usually called a TO map.
17. Translated with reference to Danielle Lecoq,"La 'mappemonde' du De Arca Noe Mystica de Hugues de Saint-Victor (1128–29)," *Géographie du monde au Moyen âge et à la Renaissance*, ed. Monique Pelletier (Paris: Editions du comité des Travaux Historiques et Scientifiques, 1989), Lecoq's reading (op. cit., p. 20) of Hugh de Saint-Victor, PL 176, col. 677D–678AB.
18. See in particular Jill Tattersall's article that views a move to the Orient as simply a "shift of perspectives"—Jill Tattersall, "Shifting Perspectives and the Illusion of Reality in Aucassin et Nicolette," *French Studies* 38 (3) (1984), p. 263.
19. Sénac, op. cit., p. 87.
20. Eugene Vance, *Mervelous Signals* (Lincoln: University of Nebraska Press, 1986).
21. A. Micha, "En relisant 'Aucassin et Nicolette'" *De la Chanson de geste au roman* (Geneva: Droz, 1976), pp. 465–478.
22. *Le conte de Floire et Blancheflor*, ed. J.-L. Leclanche, modern French translation

with foreword and notes (Paris: Champion, 1986), p. 16, note 2.
  23. All citations taken from *Conte de Floire et Blancheflor*, ed. J.-L. Leclanche (Paris: Champion CFMA, 1983), line 60.
  24. Leclanche 1986, op. cit., p. 19, note 9.
  25. Ibid., p. 31, note 26.
  26. Leclanche 1983, op. cit., line 1392.
  27. Leclanche 1986, op. cit., p. 31, note 26.
  28. Leclanche 1983, op. cit., line 1503.
  29. Ibid., line 122.
  30. Ibid., line 322.
  31. Ibid., line 1392.
  32. Ibid., lines 519, 1312, 1404, etc.
  33. Ibid., line 1369.
  34. Ibid., line 2008.
  35. Ibid., lines 2034–40.
  36. Ibid., lines 1409–12.
  37. Christine Deluz explores the various views of the Earthly Paradise and its presence/inaccessibility. Christiane Deluz, "Le paradis terrestre, image de l'orient lointain dans quelques documents géographiques médiévaux," *Images et signes de l'Orient dans l'Occident médiéval*, ed. Arrouye. Sénéfiance 11 (Aix-en-Provence: Université de Provence, 1982), pp. 145–161.
  38. *Aucassin et Nicolette*, ed. J. Dufournet (Paris: Champion CFMA, 1973), laisse XXX, lines 8–9.
  39. María Rosa Menocal, "Signs of the Times: Self, Other and History in Aucassin et Nicolette," *Romanic Review* 80(4) (1989), pp. 497–511.
  40. *Aucassin et Nicolette*, op. cit., laisse XXXIV, lines 10–12.
  41. Ibid., laisse XXXVI, line 2.
  42. Ibid., laisse XXXVI, lines 9–11.
  43. Ibid., laisse XXXVII, lines 6–9.
  44. Ibid., line 1141.
  45. Eugene Vance, "Aucassin et Nicolette as a Medieval Comedy of *Signification and Exchange*," *The Nature of Medieval Narrative*, ed. Grunmann-Gaudet (Lexington, KY: French Forum, 1980), p 60. Vance echoes Tony Hunt in this opinion. Hunt writes, "Ce qui importe c'est qu'Aucassin reste toujours le même. Il n'y a pas de changement dans sa conduite, ni dans celle de son amie non plus," Tony Hunt, "La Parodie médiévale : le cas d'Aucassin et Nicolette," *Romania* 100 (1979), p. 373.
  46. W. W. Kibler, "Archetypal Imagery in Floire et Blancheflor," *Romance Quarterly* 35 (1988), p. 19, note 9.
  47. *Aucassin et Nicolette*, op. cit., lines 23–26.
  48. Jean Favier, *Les Grandes découvertes d'Alexandre à Magellen* (Paris: Fayard, 1991), p. 118.

7. Transitional Figures

> Et lorsque je tente d'aller voir, derrière ce que je crois être le point, là-bas dans l'autre monde, d'où ça me regarde, c'est moi-même, et notre monde, à la fin, que je retrouve.[1]

The theme of travel between East and West remained popular throughout the Middle Ages precisely because it enabled a glimpse into what relationships were and could be. The earlier medieval author fantasized total defeat of the Saracen and the incorporation through marriage of Saracen women as a final defeat of the Infidel; the physical boundary did not exist in these stories so travel was easily effected. The poet dreamed of the possible yet-impossible unification of two lovers made distant by both physical and cultural boundaries; here, the demarcation between lands proved insurmountable and travel was difficult or impossible. The romance author saw the obstacles in the way of intercultural love, and yet managed to overcome them. The battle between two armies that wins for the epic hero his or her mate turns to an interior struggle, often a journey to self-discovery. Travel has become important only as a means of eventually finding oneself.

The Orient, already the land of amorous encounter in the work of the troubadours and the later *chansons de geste*, becomes in romance a space where gender and race become fluid. In this space where resemblance and reality no longer coincide, the traveler is free to reinvent himself or herself at the most basic levels of race and gender. Lovers cast off and take on identities seemingly at will in order to achieve their goals. In examining the similarities and differences between expressions of self-identity in the romances of *Aucassin et Nicolette*, *Floire et Blancheflor*, and *Lion de Bourges*, shifting perspectives of the Saracen-Christian relationship become evident.

What does it mean for a character to be perceived as of the opposite gender in a medieval text? Allen Frantzen's article on cross-dressing female saints claims that "Switches of gender identity are opportunities to explore the meaning of gender itself as a performative category that interrogates the nature positions of male and female that are opposed to centers of gender anxiety."² Cross-dressing, then, puts an emphasis on the fluidity of gender. Perceived gender is simply a performance whose effect is to call into question the positioning of male and female as opposites, looking instead at those areas of overlap, where the male and the female intersect. In the one-sex model of human sexuality espoused by Western society from antiquity until the nineteenth century, the female is simply an underdeveloped, insufficient male. Women, according to Galen, were men whose sexual organs had failed to drop from the internal cavity due to a lack of body heat.³ Examples of half-men/half-women, or persons who had developed further than women but not as far as men, were commonplace as examples to prove this one-sex theory. Gender switching in a medieval text thus further illustrates the male-female continuum and the ability to exist at degrees along the sexual spectrum.

Studies of cross-dressing in the medieval literary text have echoed Frantzen's findings for the saints' lives. In the German and French traditions, a particularly intriguing genre is that of the abandoned wife who must cross-dress in order to regain her husband's love. The typical challenge might involve a series of quests that the wife must accomplish, like getting the husband's ring and becoming pregnant by him. Since the husband is unwilling to interact with his wife, he assumes these tasks to be impossible and considers himself rid of his unwanted wife. Within the female sphere of the home, these functions would be impossible, but by taking on a male disguise, the wife is able to leave the home and trick her husband into compliance. Valerie Hotchkiss notes that these literary heroines who take on masculine disguise "achieve a twofold success: they prove their ability to survive and even flourish in male spheres, and, moreover, they ultimately conform to accepted models of femininity in medieval literature."⁴ Only by taking on the guise of a male character can the wife perform the seemingly impossible feats that her husband has decreed for him to take her back. In renouncing her sexuality she is in fact able to regain it legitimately.

The same scenario does not hold true for the male cross-dresser in medieval literature. As Michèle Perret has noted, for men the result and/or goal of their transvestism is to gain sexual access to women,⁵ as found in the theme of the male in nun's garb who satisfies both himself and the presumably inaccessible women who surround him. The temporary renunciation of sexual activity, however, is the goal or result of female transvestism, as the cross-dresser may use her disguise to travel safely through the public sphere. Vern L. Bullough suggests that male cross-dressers were regarded with hostility for "acting in any way that could be interpreted as feminine."⁶ While male and female cross-dressers occupy the same ambiguous zone on the gender continuum, they do so with differing motivations and results.

Just as literary characters cross gender lines, they often disrupt class lines. The abandoned wife often takes on the guise of a servant in order to gain access to her husband's entourage and accomplish her required tasks. As Hotchkiss remarks, however, the husband is most likely to recognize the innate nature of the servant's nobility,[7] though he remains ignorant as to her sexual identity. Since sexuality was conceived of as a continuum, the effeminate man or the masculine woman do not seem to raise any speculations. Questions of class, however, seem more cut and dried. Though one could attempt to disguise one's class, the inner self could not be suppressed forever.

The texts of *Aucassin et Nicolette*, *Floire et Blancheflor*, and *Lion de Bourges*[8] share these general characteristics of the cross-dressing protagonist. Like the abandoned wife, Nicolette takes on male garb to regain her love, Aucassin. Alis of *Lion de Bourges* offers a slight variation on the theme, having been captured and separated from husband and child rather than abandoned. These two women renounce their sexuality, refusing marriage and fighting off rapists, in order to regain their social status as women. Floire, in contrast, as other male cross-dressers, enters the female world in order to make love to Blancheflor. He is mistakenly perceived to be a woman at the very moment that he is able to consummate his love for Blancheflor. All three protagonists attempt to cross class lines as well, masquerading as a minstrel, kitchen servant, and a merchant. Both Nicolette and Alis are eventually deemed to be noble outside their societies, though their origins were unclear. Floire, too, is uncovered as an impostor as he attempts to conceal his elevated background. Although their class origins are discovered, their genders are not. Nicolette and Alis are never detected as women; they determine the proper moment to reveal themselves. Floire almost passes as a woman, and would do so were it not for the extreme jealousy of his love's fiancé. Thus these cases offer further illustration of some of the generalizations already made about literary transvestism.

Yet these three texts offer something that the majority of cross-dressing tales do not. These stories involve the crossing of ethnic and social boundaries at the same time that the cross-dressing occurs. Not only must the characters "pass" as of the opposite sex, they must also negotiate cultural difference, passing (or failing to pass) as members of a different ethnic group. What is particularly interesting about these texts is that they respond directly to a concern Frantzen voices elsewhere in his article, namely the importance of examining race as well as gender. While the Old English saints' lives do not provide material for such an analysis, these French texts offer examples of gender confusion as a passport for entering the culture of another ethnic group.

Nicolette, the feisty heroine of *Aucassin et Nicolette*, lives in Biaucaire, a Christian land in medieval France. Originally Saracen, Nicolette was captured and sold to a Christian who adopted and baptized her. While the story makes clear that she was once Muslim, her exact family origins are a mystery for most of the romance. As a woman of common birth and foreign roots, she is considered unsuitable as a love interest for Aucassin, future heir of Biaucaire. Aucassin's father says the words that even Nicolette's adoptive father will repeat to the young man:

> Nicolete laise ester, que ce est une caitive qui fu amenee d'estrange terre, si l'acata li visquens de ceste vile as Sarasins, si l'amena en ceste vile, si l'a levee et bautisie et faite sa fillole, si li donra un de ces jors un baceler qui du pain li gaaignera par honor: de ce n'as tu que faire.[9]

> [Leave Nicolette alone, for she is a slave brought from a foreign land. The viscount of this town bought her from the Saracens, brought her to this town, raised her, baptized her, and made her his adoptive daughter. He will give her a young man someday who with his hard work will win her honorably. Of these things, you have no part.]

Nicolette would never be a suitable match because she represents a center of social anxiety. Her body refuses to be categorized—she is neither fully Christian nor fully Saracen. Her skin is white, yet she is an outsider. Her unknown family cannot be considered common or noble. Her entire origin is at question. Despite this, the two lovers are not easily dissuaded, for they cannot be convinced of the importance of these social categories. The story cannot be resolved until the issue of social categories is addressed.

Pirates who raid the shores of Torelore, where the lovers are living an idyllic exile, separate Aucassin and Nicolette. While Aucassin is fortuitously brought back to Biaucaire, his native country, Nicolette is whisked to Carthage, whose city walls she recognizes from her childhood. At this point she realizes that she is the daughter of the Emir, a noblewoman by any medieval standards.

But her mind is on her adoptive country and her lover Aucassin. As discussed previously, she rejects her own people as savages. At the same time that Nicolette clears up two questions about her person, that of her station (noble) and her ethnicity (Saracen), she responds by challenging all the ways in which she has been labeled. When her father tries to marry her to a noble Saracen, she flees the country, blackening her white face and cross-dressing as a minstrel. Only through this final breaking down of the categories of race and gender can Nicolette achieve her final goal—full integration into French society. She appears at the court of Biaucaire as her opposite—black, male, and of common birth—and her songs tell the story of the other Nicolette—white, female, and very noble. When she is assured of Aucassin's love for Nicolette, she removes her disguise and joins him permanently. Just as the Imaginary Jew in Clark and Sponsler's study of medieval theater represents desire and appropriation of the Other,[10] Nicolette's racial cross-dressing serves to fully reject the Saracen through that appropriation. By taking off her "real" or Saracen self, she paradoxically becomes acceptable, though she returns to the state she was when first rejected. Though Jacqueline de Weever was right to underline Nicolette's blackness,[11] her blackness served as yet another putting off or rejection of

Saracen culture.

Alis, mother of Lion in the epic *Lion de Bourges*, is Nicolette's Christian counterpart. Three thieves, who each claim the right to sleep with her, capture her. Central to their arguments about who will win her and take her home is the issue of her clothing. The first thief offers to give her luxurious clothing to the other two men in order to take her home as his lover alone:

> Je vous dont en vous part son blanc siglaton,
> Et cilz aultre compain arait son pellisson.
> Trez bien la vestirait et bel en ma maxon . . .[12]

> [I give you, for your share, her white overshirt, and this other companion will have her fur coat. I will dress her well and beautifully in my house.]

The two men are not assuaged by this offer of clothing, and in the ensuing fight over control of Alis' body, the three men kill each other. In a reversal of the offer made by the first thief, Alis undresses the thieves and dresses herself as a man in order to travel in safety:

> A ung dez laron vint qui la estoit fenis,
> Ces drap li devestit dont il esoit polis;
> La damme s'an parait et si lez ait vestis,
> En droit habit d'un homme est adont cez cors mis,
> L'espee a son costez dont li brans est forbis.
> Lors se mist a la voie per estrainge pays . . .[13]

> [She went to one of the dead thieves and took off the material with which he was dressed. The woman took it and dressed herself with it. Her body was put in the proper dress of a man, with a sword with sharpened blade at her side. And so she set out on the route to foreign lands.]

The final sentence "Lors se mist a la voie per estrainge pays" omnisciently indicates the immediate effect of cross-dressing—a trip to foreign, different lands. Alis' transvestism both enables and marks the beginning of her introduction to another culture.

Alis sets off, finding a ship that will take her to Jerusalem, where she hopes to encounter her husband and son. Destiny, or the Virgin Mary as Alis believes, has other plans for Alis, and her ship is tossed off course by a storm, arriving in Muslim Spain rather than the intended Jerusalem. The text relates that Alis is still dressed as a man, and specifies that she has colored her skin:

> En guise d'omme estoit la duchesse paree:
> Bien sambloit ionnes hons, la faice ot colloree.[14]

> [The duchess was dressed in the disguise of a man. She really looked like a young man—she had colored her face.]

Like Nicolette, Alis must change both clothing and skin color in order to be perceived as a Saracen man.

Though she begins in the kitchens of the Emir, Alis soon proves her prowess and intelligence. She integrates fully into the court, pretending to be a pagan herself and learning "sarracenois" fluently.

> Car antandre faisoit qu'elle estoit renoye,
> Et qu'elle ne creoit Dieu n'en sainte Mairie;
> Du langaige au paien fut bientost ansignie....[15]
>
> [She made it understood that she had rejected her faith and that she did not believe in God or in Saint Mary. She was soon well versed in the pagan language.]

No task is too small or too large for her capable attention. She excels both in the kitchen and at knightly pursuits, saving the Emir's kingdom from threat of destruction. None of the Saracen men have enough backbone to counter the challenge of the evil pagan giant Lucien who is determined to marry the Emir's daughter Florie against her will. Joan of Arc *avant la lettre*, Alis, busy in the kitchen, hears a voice telling her that God wants her to meet Lucien's challenge. She does so with great success, provoking the love of the Emir's daughter in the process. Before that abomination could take place, Alis, now indispensable to the Emir, reveals her secret to the Emir. While this stops his daughter's courtship, it inflames the passion of the Emir himself who determines to marry Alis. Fleeing the court of the Emir, Alis manages to keep herself for the father of *Lion de Bourges*.

Unlike the cross-dressing heroines studied by Michèle Perret,[16] no linguistic confusion results from Alis' transvestism. Adjectives and nouns are masculine when others refer to Alis, for they perceive her to be a man. She, too, refers to herself as a man while speaking to others, using male-gendered language. In fact, she takes on the history, though not the name, of her much-beloved husband when she recounts her past. But the text always keeps her real sex evident to both Alis and the reader/listener. Mindful of her own body, Alis knows that her feats of strength come not so much from within as from the aid of God and the Virgin.

> N'est pas euvre de femme ou me sus atornee!
> Mais pués que Dieu le vuelt, et la vertu nommee,
> Je ferai son volloir huy en cest jornee.[17]
>
> [This is not woman's work that I have directed myself toward! But since God wishes it and virtue has named it, I will do his will this day.]

Rather amusingly, even at the height of the epic battle Alis wages with the giant, she is referred to as either "la damme" or "la duchesse."

Alis' testing in Saracen lands makes her the suitable mother for an extraordinary hero, Lion de Bourges. Her position is unique—the most beautiful of women as well as the most valiant and courageous of men. This paradox, the inability to cast her as either male or female but as extraordinary male and female, sets a difficult standard for medieval women. The only woman suitable for the mother of a hero is completely inimitable. Like the Virgin Mary who embodied the paradox of being at once mother and virgin, Alis must incorporate conflicting roles, that of male and female. Not insignificantly, Alis invokes the Virgin repeatedly in the text. Alis is admirable precisely because she could not possibly exist. The author insists on her feminine nature through pronoun usage to remind the reader/listener that this is not a real knight. Her occupation of a position of authority is compromised in that she has crossed ethnic boundaries. The author can allow Alis to best all the Saracen knights, but it is unlikely that the audience would have accepted her defeat of all Christian knights. Likewise, Alis never marries a Saracen. Her trip to Saracen lands does not lead to the permanent integration found in either *Aucassin et Nicolette* or *Floire et Blancheflor*.

As a counter to the two women, a final example of gender bending in medieval romance involves a male, Floire of the twelfth-century *Floire et Blancheflor*. In contrast to the women, Floire does not consciously take on the attributes of the opposite sex (perhaps due to the stigma of being feminine referred to by Bullough), but the author of the text makes plain that Floire could easily be mistaken for a girl. Floire and Blancheflor are born on the same day, he of a noble Saracen woman and she of the enslaved Christian servant of that same noblewoman. From the beginning, the similarities between the two children are stressed, with the femininity of the two always at the forefront. Their names, for example, refer to the flowers of "Pâques Fleuries," or Palm Sunday, the day on which the children were born. Floire, a name more commonly feminine than masculine, signifies from the outset the importance of Christianity, even though the boy Floire is a Saracen from Muslim Spain. The two children are brought up identically by the Christian servant, though the young Floire sent to be nursed by a Saracen "Une paiienne l'alaitoit, car lor lois l'autre refusoit."[18] [A pagan nursed him because their laws refused the other]. This mother's milk, one Saracen and one Christian, reminds the reader of the sole difference between the two, one of religion and/or ethnicity. Yet from the outset the gender and ethnic difference between the two children are intentionally blurred.

As the love between the two children grows, the father of Floire, realizing the unsuitability of the Christian Blancheflor for his future heir, decides to separate the two children. While he originally plans to kill Blancheflor, his queen convinces him to sell the girl into slavery. When Floire learns of the treachery, he vows to set out and recover his beloved. At this point, his femininity becomes crucial to the success of his endeavor. Not sure where to look for his love, Floire is continually pointed in the proper direction because he looks so much like Blancheflor, who passed that way earlier. One hostess remarks:

> el vos resanle, en moie foi,
> bien poés estre d'un eage,
> si vos resanle du visage.[19]

[She looks like you, by my faith. You could be the same age. She looks so much like you in the face.]

Yet another hostess comments that he must be Blancheflor's twin sister "Jou cuit qu'ele est sa suer jumele : / tel vis, tel cors et tel sanlant"[20] [I think that she is her twin sister—same face, same body, same appearance].

When Floire finally arrives at the tower where Blancheflor is being held in the harem of the Emir of Babiloine, he hides himself in a basket of flowers and eventually reaches the room of his beloved. The two live in sexual bliss until the day that Blancheflor is late getting out of bed and the Emir's chamberlain goes to wake her. He sees the two sleeping together, and mistakes the boy for Blancheflor's best friend, Gloris. The text makes plain the grounds for confusing Floire with the young girl:

> vis li est qu'il i a veü
> Blanceflor et bele Gloris.
> Por coi ne li fust il avis ?
> K'a face n'a menton n'avoit
> barbe, ne grenons n'i paroit :
> en la tor n'avoit damoisele
> qui de visage fust plus bele.[21]

[He believes that he saw Blancheflor and beautiful Gloris there. Why should he not be of this opinion? The face and chin had neither beard nor sideburns. In the tower there was no young lady who had a more beautiful face.]

The chamberlain hesitates to wake them because he finds the scene so touching. The evident sexuality between the two, because it is perceived as between two women, does not upset the servant. He reports to the Emir:

> "Sire, merveilles ai veü !
> Ainc mais si grans amors ne fu
> com a Blanceflor vers Gloris
> et ele a li, ce m'est avis.
>
> Ensanle dorment doucement,
> acolé s'ont estroitement,
> et bouce a bouce et face a face
> s'ont acolé, et brace a brace . . .
> Molt lor siet a gesir ensanle."[22]

[Sire, I have seen a marvelous thing. There was never a greater love than that of Blancheflor for Gloris and she for her, in my opinion. Together they are sweetly sleeping, hugged tightly to each other, mouth to mouth, face to face they are wrapped in each other's arms . . . It suits them well to lie together.]

Unfortunately for Floire, Gloris is with the Emir when the chamberlain makes his report.

When the Emir rushes to discover who is lying with his betrothed, he too believes Floire to be a woman, though his excessive jealousy gives him doubts. The Emir repeats the observation that, aside from Blancheflor, there is no woman more beautiful than Floire in his harem. He commands that the shirts be ripped from the two girls to uncover their breasts, and only then is Floire known to be a man. At the trial that follows, the two lovers are spared death only by the pity evoked by their great beauty and their efforts to save each other at the expense of their own life. Rather than defending his love with arms, as most medieval heroes would do, Floire notes that as a man he should die first. Blancheflor will not allow this, and the two fight to sacrifice themselves for each other. The two lovers win pardon through their ultimate femininity, portrayed as sobbing, abject, and above all beautiful in the face of death. Once released, Floire converts himself and his subjects to Christianity, he marries Blancheflor, and the two rule his now (conveniently) dead father's kingdom.

The examples of Floire, Alis, and Nicolette illustrate the ability for members of one sex to be perceived as of the opposite sex. Perhaps even more so in the Middle Ages than in later times, the one-sex view of gender enabled characters to move fluidly between male and female. Living as a male when one was female did not call into question the ultimate femininity of either Alis or Nicolette. Likewise, despite his formerly feminine characteristics, Floire becomes a great ruler of a vast empire. These stories appear to interrogate the performative aspect of gender, and their conclusions challenge the idea that only men can do men things (like fight and take initiative) and only women can excel in womanly areas (like beauty and sensitivity).

Once the category of sex has been broken down, what Marjorie Garber terms a "crisis of category"[23] results —now that one category has been questioned, all other categories lose their ability to fully describe. Put another way, as Myra Jehlen has noted, "it is logically impossible to interrogate gender—to transform it from axiom to object of scrutiny and critical term—without also interrogating race and class."[24] And this is precisely the ultimate goal of these three texts. Once one category has been challenged, it becomes easier to accept movement in other categories. Like gender, race appears to lie upon a continuum, at least superficially. Thus Alis passes as male in order to become Saracen. The author shows that the best Saracen knight is actually a Christian woman, thus minimizing the Saracen threat. Alis must cross both ethnic and gender boundaries in order to make the author's ultimate point of the superiority of Lion de Bourges and, ultimately, the French. Nicolette switches back and forth from black male to white female. If she can accomplish this feat, she can easily go from commoner to noble and convert to Christianity as well. Through the ultimate fluidity of her character, she is able to change from someone totally unsuitable for the wife of a French ruler to the perfect mate and mother of future heirs. Floire's ambiguous gender enables his pardon and ultimate conversion. If the reader can accept him as female, surely he can be accepted as a mighty Christian ruler as well. Each character's chameleon-like gender and character prove to be his or her ultimate strengths.

Despite the gender and ethnic switching evident in these texts, the Middle Ages can hold no claim for greater sexual or racial tolerance than subsequent periods.[25] While the lines between the sexes and races are blurred, there is no middle ground that can be permanently occupied. The exceptional qualities of these characters make them as rare as the half-men/half-women used to illustrate Galen's theories in the Middle Ages. Furthermore, in the case of these romances, the truth will out; innate gender and ethnic categories will prevail. If gender is a performative category, so then is race. Ethnic anxiety is confronted, and fears are put to rest as characters reject multiple ethnic identities in favor of integration. Far from advocating relative or equal merit to ethnic or sexual states, the three texts underline both the cultural superiority of the French and the supremacy of the masculine over the feminine. In the end, all characters are returned to their proper, unambiguous roles, firmly entrenched in Western patriarchy and nobility. The boundaries which once seemed so fluid and easily crossed are in the final analysis yet more firmly entrenched.

Much like the one-sex view of human sexuality that the medieval West espoused, a one-race view of mankind emerges. A character can switch from Saracen to Christian, apparently convincingly, with the help of a few well-mixed herbs. Language is learned effortlessly. However, just as a female was an underdeveloped male, so the black Saracen was a white Christian *manqué*. Some persons, like Nicolette and Floire, could achieve "full Christianity" because they were from the start closer to the Christian physical ideal. In the end, all characters are placed in their proper, unambiguous roles, firmly entrenched in Western patriarchy and nobility. The boundaries which once seemed so fluid and easily crossed are in the final analysis yet more firmly entrenched.

Recalling the move toward obstacle and rejection of Saracen-Christian relationships in medieval romance, the role of gender in these cases furthers this observation. While the Saracen boy Floire in the end overcomes his femininity and his Scarcenness to become a great Christian ruler, neither Nicolette nor Alis ever fully belong to the masculine world. Their femininity, like their race, is hidden so that they can survive in a threatening world. Floire, on the other hand, makes no effort to hide or change his gender; he simply moves from the feminine to the masculine. He "develops" or finds his full potential, whereas Nicolette and Alis are covering up their ultimate selves. They may masquerade as men, but as Alis eloquently noted, "N'est pas euvre de femme ou me sus atornee!" [This is not women's work to which I have committed myself!]. Self-identity—ethnic, religious and sexual—is established in the Orient in the more culturally positive *Floire et Blancheflor*. The more pessimistic, later works see travel and cultural penetration as a time of potential discovery, but where the discovery must be carefully hidden until return to one's country of origin.

Relationships between Christians and Muslims in these texts mirror the changes that took place between Christians and Muslims in society. Nicolette and Blancheflor portray a period of questioning of the ability for two different peoples to coexist. Unlike Guibourc, who at her début marries Guillaume d'Orange with apparently no disapproval, Nicolette and Blancheflor both meet with the initial disapproval of the potential fathers-in-law. In both cases, the father/rulers threaten to kill the woman-Other who entices their sons. Society does not immediately accept these women. Only after a period of departure and a series of trials to prove their mettle can the Other come back and claim her place. Perhaps most importantly, the objecting fathers conveniently disappear from the scene before her return.

While both women are eventually accepted, it requires the death of the father, who in Lacanian terms represents law and the structure of society, to allow her entrance. María Rosa Menocal points out that, "The fact that Nicolette is a Saracen is as irrelevant for the younger generation as it is an absolute obstacle for the older one."[26] While Menocal reads this as an uplifting example of how Christians longed for and achieved a measure of coexistence, the lesson, in light of earlier, non-problematic relationships like Guibourc and Guillaume, is much more pessimistic. Integration requires the overturning of the existing structure of society, which makes for a good tale, but like Torelore, could hardly be confused with reality.

Alis, who comes along after the death of Llull and the abandoning of hope for conversion of the Saracen, paints an even dimmer picture. Her forays into Saracen land result in absolutely no permanent bonds. Even la fille du comte de Ponthieu married a Saracen and recanted her faith, even if only to deny it later. But Alis lives among the Saracens without ever, even for a second, losing sight of her eventual goal: reintegration in French society. She is a tourist in Saracen lands, albeit the opposite of the Ugly American. Learning the language and blending into the scenery around her paradoxically serves to allow her to distinguish herself; with her skills at cultural integration she manages to protect her all-important sexuality. The future mother of a Christian hero, she never engages in cross-cultural sexual activity, unlike Blancheflor, Nicolette and la fille du comte de Ponthieu.

Geographical images of the Orient show as well the ever-shifting view of the East. No tale illustrates this movement better than that of Prester John. The story began in the twelfth century, telling of a mythical priest who ruled a marvelous land of incredible richness. A devout Christian, Prester John controlled a vast amount of land toward the East, and with his help, the Christians could finally and definitively defeat the Infidel. The search for this ultimate ally was on; voyagers recounted their efforts to encounter the king for centuries to come. The legend continued throughout the Middle Ages, into the fifteenth century, when certain travelers claimed to have finally found the magnificent court of Prester John. The changing role of Prester John and his kingdom tell much of the changes affecting Muslim-Christian relations during this period.

Prester John appears on the scene for the first time in the chronicle of Otto of Freising, who tells of the crushing defeat of the Seljouk chiefs around 1145 by a Nestorian king, *Presbyter Johannes*. The real origin of the legend surrounding Prester John, however, comes from a Latin letter written around 1150, allegedly by the Prester himself, to the leaders of Christianity—the Byzantine emperor, Manuel Comnenus, Frederick Barbarossa, and Pope Alexander III. Prester John announces in the letter his intention of crusading against the Infidel, and he requests the assistance of the heads of Christianity. This fictitious letter is clearly aimed at the unification of the disparate elements of the Christian Empires. Prester John serves as facilitator of cooperation among the three leaders. His letter encourages them to see the Infidel as the focus of their attentions. With cooperation, the Infidel can be overcome and the Holy Land recaptured. Crusade then serves as unification of Christendom.

The *mappaemundi* of the twelfth to fifteenth centuries convey this sense of Christendom as a united whole. The world is divided into continents, Asia, Africa and Europe, with Jerusalem occupying the center of the map (see figures 1 and 2). By framing the entire world within the Christian context, Jerusalem in the center, the Earthly Paradise and Hell at the extreme margins of the map, medieval mapmakers imply that everyone is potentially a part of the Christian community. Iain Higgins interprets these maps:

> Latin Christendom as represented on these maps can be thought of as being at once an imagined and an imaginary religious community—that is a real community of believers projecting an image of their communion well past its actual boundaries in the world to a point at which it no longer has any basis in reality.[27]

The community of believers played a major role in imagining one's society and world in the Middle Ages. However, this community changed in scope and perception over the course of the centuries. As such, moments of self-identity found in medieval literature (and of particular interest to this study, when self-definition was achieved through contrast with the Other) reflect these differences in world-view. Representations of the kingdom of Prester John mirror changes in medieval thought concerning the Christian community.

In the thirteenth-century Yale manuscript of the *Lettre du Prêtre Jean*, the Western Christian community takes precedent over the sense of Christianity as a whole. This Old French version of the letter from Prester John to the Byzantine Emperor contains the same utopist description of the land of Prester John. His country is devoid of vice and full of luxury and natural wonder. The Yale manuscript, after completing this highly appealing description of a veritable paradise on Earth, includes the story of an Englishman who has actually visited Prester John's realm. A 100-line addition tells of a pilgrim William of Ver, who made extensive travels in the Orient and ended up

Transitional Figures 95

in Prester John's court. The inhabitants welcome him and offer him luxurious accommodations, should he wish to remain in their land. The text, however, makes explicit his refusal of their generous offer: "Mes il ne volt faire niënt, Ke il ama trop tendrement Engleterre dunt il est niez" [But he did not wish at all to do it for he loved England, where he was born, too much.][28] His situation is compared to that of a caged bird who, though well-treated, will return to his home in the wild if allowed to escape:

> Le russinol bien resembla
> Qui fors del bois est pigun pris
> E puis en kage enclos e mis:
> Ja tant ne sera danzelez,
> Suuef nuri ne bien amez
> Ke, s'il pot eissir hors de la kage,
> Tuit dreit en ault vers le boscage.[29]

> [He was like the nightengale who is trapped and taken from the woods and enclosed in a cage. Any young man, no matter how well he is nourished and loved, if he is able to leave the cage, he will go straight-away to the woods.]

The land of Prester John, which combines both marvel and Christianity, holds no sway over the West. Whereas earlier marvelous lands were unsuitable due to their pagan religion, this land is undesirable simply because it is not England. A sense of nationalism replaces the notion of the community of believers, underscoring that there really is no place like home. The author of this addendum reflects the changes of a century and a half, when Fulcher of Chartre, marveling at the Orient as an eye-witness of the First Crusade, wrote in his *Historia Hierosolymitana* of 1127 that:

> For we who were Occidentals have now become Orientals. He who was a Roman or a Frank has in this land been made into a Galilean or a Palestinian. . . . We have already forgotten the places of our birth; already these are unknown to many of us or not mentioned any more . . .[30]

What was once conceivable as suitable for appropriation and integration has already been relegated to the permanent position of marvelous and Other. As the Holy Land is appropriated, the land of Paradise and wonder must move elsewhere, to the Indes of Prester John or, later, Ethiopia.

The strange text of the *Fille du comte de Ponthieu* shows a different take on the theme of Saracen-Christian interaction. In a scene of remarkable violence, the *fille* is raped by a band of thieves in front of her injured and bound husband. She tries to kill him, freeing him instead. When her father hears the story, he throws her out to sea in a wooden barrel. Rescued by merchants, she is given to the Sultan of Aumarie who converts, weds and cherishes her. Her father, husband and brother, on pilgrimage because of their guilty feelings about having disposed of the *fille*, land in Aumarie thanks to a fortuitous storm. The *fille*, finally recognizing them, saves them from execution and eventually flees with them back to France. She takes her son by the sultan with her to France but must leave behind her daughter. The daughter, according to the text, will become the grandmother of the courtois Turk, Saladin.

The story first appeared in the thirteenth century, where the text fills in little more detail than the summary just presented. The *fille's* motivations for trying to kill her husband never surface. Nor does the justification for the father's apparently excessive retribution. The *fille* lives in Aumarie surrounded by luxury and respect, and her integration becomes evident in that she masters the Arabic language and takes on the religion of her husband. Thus her return to France with her previously rather ungrateful family remains something of a mystery.

A fifteenth-century version of the text, however, shows how the changing view of the Saracen affected the literature of the later Middle Ages. In this text, all motivations become clearly defined. The fille tries to kill her husband because she is so ashamed of being dishonored that she wants to leave no witnesses, and she plans to kill herself as soon as she has dispatched her husband. Her father, finding his daughter so dishonored, punishes her with what amounts to the death penalty in the hopes of avoiding damage to the family reputation. In the court of Aumarie, the fille does not truly convert to Islam, but she pretends to do so in order to avoid being taken by force, as earlier experience has shown that to be quite undesirable. The chance to return to France with her family provides a fairy-tale ending, where all is righted in the end.

Certainly, a large part of the *amplificatio* in the fifteenth-century version is due to the desire to expand upon an already-popular story. The fifteenth-century text is inserted in the *Jean d'Avesnes* epic-romance trilogy, with the story of Jean d'Avesnes explaining the origin of the *fille* (he is her grandfather), followed by the *Fille du comte de Ponthieu*, and, finally, terminated by *Saladin*, which takes the story of the *fille's* great-grandson and tells of his interaction with the French on crusade.

By the thirteenth century, the French captive is no longer able to convert an entire country and live in peace and love with a well-intentioned Saracen. The call of France and the innate Frenchness of the *fille* win out over any social or cultural ties. The *fille* remains afraid that her French relatives will persecute her should she return to France, making them promise to keep their word that they will cherish her:

> "Seigneur, jou voel ke vous recordés les paroles qui dites furent, car encor ai jou bien pooir du retourner, se jou voel." Et il disent: "Dame, nous ne disimes coze que nous ne voellons bien tenir."[31]

> ["My lords, I wish for you to remember the words that you said, for I am still very afraid of returning, as I wish." And they said, "Lady, we do not say things that we do not mean to do."]

In a remarkable show of sensitivity, the *fille* also procurs their assurance that her son by the Sultan will be well treated. She sends back the Sultan's ship and belongings, stating that, . . . "j'ai molt tolu au soudant quant jou li ai tolu mon cors et son fil, ne plus de sez cozes jou ne li bé a tolir"[32] [I have taken much from the sultan when I took from him my body and his son. I have no desire to steal any more of his things]. The *fille's* continued fear of her own people and her recognition that she and her children are loved and well treated by the Sultan play a delicate balance in her decision to return to her own people. She wants to return to who and what she was, but she also sees that her situation in Aumarie could be much better than a return to neglect and/or condemnation in Ponthieu.

The homecoming scene according to the fifteenth-century text illustrates the change in tone of the entire text. The *fille* instructs the sultan's sailors to take her to a land where she will understand the language, that is, the port of Brandis in France. She again makes the husband and father agree that they will cherish her, but the tone is not one of fear but of renewal:

> . . . la dame moult joieuse prist terre et vault savoir a son pere et a son mary s'ilz vouloient tenir leur convenance. A laquelle ilz affermerent par renovacion de sermens qu'ils ameroient mieulx mourir que pencer envers icelle de dire ne proposer nulle tache de blasme ne laidure.[33]

> [The lady joyfully landed and wished to know from her father and husband if they would keep their promises. The reaffirmed by oath to her that they would rather die than think or say about her any bit of blame or ugliness.]

Her dispatch of the sultan's ship changes from an attempt to do right by the sultan to the method for her to send the message of her defiance to her former captor. She tells the sailors:

> O vous, qui de chetive et dampnable servitude avés amenee en ceste terre la dame administree de plusieurs temptacions, vous vous en retournerés au soudan vostre sire et luy dirés de par moy que je l'ay desnué de mon corps et de la conversation de son tres amé filz par la recouvrance de ces trois prisonniers, desquelz vecy mon pere, ce gentil chevalier est mon mary et ce vassal cy est mon frere, et pour ce, ralés vous ent, disans que je me suis reduite a ma primiere loy et que l'en ne me verra jamés par dela, se mervilleuse fortune ne m'y remaine.[34]

> [O you, who have brought to this land in base and damnable servitude the woman overtaken with many temptations, you return to the sultan, your sire, and say to him on my part that I have taken away from him my body and the company of his much-loved son through the recovery of these three prisoners, one if which is my father, this kind knight is my husband, and this vassal is my brother, and for that, get going, saying that I have

returned to my first law and that no one will see me outside of that unless a marvelous destiny overtakes me.]

Her return to her "primiere loy" denotes a natural, perhaps innate, code of rules and life that are consistent with being French. Her return to Frenchness is both natural and desirable, and the time she has spent as "Other" becomes cast as a period of servitude and subjugation to an unnatural law. The split between Muslim and Christian is complete; natural law dictates that one is born to a proper culture and switching cultures perverts the order of things.

The third text of the trilogy, *Saladin*, goes one step further, clearly indicating the cultural superiority of the French. In the text, Saladin seduces the Queen of France. Drawn to the chivalrous life of the French knights, he goes as far as having himself knighted. Just as the French had given up hope of ever conquering the Holy Land, *Saladin* has the French effectively conquering the Turk who took Jerusalem from them. Saladin's roots and natural yearnings can be attributed to the Frenchness of his great-grandmother. Her essence has been passed on (triumphing over the weaker essence of the sultan's people), creating a need to belong to the French community. He desires that which the French desire. All that is admirable in him (the historical accounts of the crusade show that Saladin was much praised by the Christians due to his courteous nature) can be traced back to his French forebears, Jean d'Avesnes in particular.

Self-definition, initiated through contact with the Orient but accomplished in the country of origin, holds its place as a dominant literary theme in the thirteenth through fifteenth centuries. Geography is destiny in that travel is the only way for characters to find loves, mend broken lives and understand themselves. As *Floire et Blancheflor* shows us, the Orient holds the place of both wonder and delight, as well as the locus of perversion. This duality continues throughout the Middle Ages, as the French imagination deals with various situations arising from the contact between Christianity and Islam. As the physical threat of the Saracen, so strong in the *Chanson de Roland* and *Gormont et Isembart*, diminishes, the French medieval text turns to the "nature as destiny" view of Saracen-Christian relations. Integration, possible though not without difficulty in *Floire et Blancheflor* and *Aucassin et Nicolette*, becomes unnatural by the time of the *Fille du comte de Ponthieu*. Travel has altered in essence, providing not the introduction to a new culture, but rather a neutral location for two parties within the same culture, the *fille* and her family for example, to work out their differences and return to peaceful coexistence.

The texts discussed in this chapter can each be rightly considered unusual. Perhaps the most exemplary in its uniqueness, *Aucassin et Nicolette* is the only example of a *chantefable* in French literary history. The tension evoked as the writer tried to reconcile changing literary convention manifests itself in the alternation of prose and lyric. The parodic element of *Aucassin et Nicolette* lies not in the theme explored and rejected, the attempt to integrate two cultural traditions, but rather in the form of the hybrid-genre text itself. The lyric inserts serve to underline the impossibility of lyric desire for the Other. Conversely, the happily-ever-after ending of epic romance (or even *Floire et Blancheflor*) cannot hold sway over the text, either. By alternating between these two generic traditions, the author attempts to reconcile desire and integration, but the text can only accomplish this purpose in erasing Nicolette's difference, thus presaging the cynicism of later texts featuring the Christian-Saracen couple.

NOTES

1. Alain Grosrichard, *Structure du sérail: la fiction du despotisme asiatique dans l'Occident classique* (Paris: Éditions du Seuil, 1979), p. 33.
2. Allen Frantzen, "When Women Aren't Enough," *Speculum*. 68 (2) (1993), p. 460.
3. Thomas Laqueur's *Making Sex* (Cambridge: Harvard UP, 1990) offers an excellent summary and analysis of the one-sex view of gender in the Middle Ages. See in particular Chapter 2, "Destiny is Anatomy."
4. Valerie Hotchkiss, "Gender Transgression and the Abandoned Wife," *Gender Rhetorics: Postures of Dominance and Submission in History*, ed. Richard C. Trexler (Binghamton, NY: Center for Medieval Texts and Studies, 1994), p. 218.
5. Michele Perret, "Travesties et Transsexuelles: Yde, Silence, Grisandole, Blanchandine," *Romance Notes* 25(3) (1984–85), p. 329.
6. Vern L. Bullough, "On Being Male in the Middle Ages," *Medieval Masculinities: Regarding Men in the Middle Ages*, ed. Clare Lees (Minneapolis: University of Minnesota Press, 1994), p. 36.
7. Hotchkiss, op. cit., p. 212.
8. Citations from the following edition of this text: *Lion de Bourges: poème épique du XIVe siècle*, ed. W. W. Kibler, Picheret, Fenster (Geneva: Droz, 1980).
9. *Aucassin et Nicolette*, ed. J. Dufournet, (Paris: Champion CFMA, 1973), II, lines 28–33.
10. Robert L. A. Clark and Claire Sponsler, "Othered Bodies: Racial Cross-Dressing in the Mistere de la Sainte Hostie and the Croxton Play of the Sacrament," *Journal of Medieval and Early Modern Studies* 29 (1) (1999), p. 81. These two authors discuss the recuperative process of Nicolette's cross-dressing in another article, Robert L.A. Clark and Claire Sponsler, "Queer Play: the Cultural Work of Crossdressing in Medieval Drama," *New Literary History* 28 (2) (1997), pp. 319–44.
11. Jacqueline de Weever, "Nicolette's Blackness: Lost in Translation," *Romance Notes* 34 (1994), pp. 317–25.
12. *Lion de Bourges: poème épique du XIVe siècle*, ed. W. W. Kibler, Picheret, Fenster. 2 vols. (Geneva: Droz, 1980), lines 631–33.
13. Ibid., lines 667–72.
14. Ibid., lines 758–59.

15. Ibid., lines 787–89.
16. Michèle Perret, op. cit., pp. 328–40.
17. *Lion de Bourges*, op. cit., lines 1662–64.
18. *Conte de Floire et Blancheflor*, ed. J.-L. Leclanche (Paris: Champion CFMA, 1983), lines 183–4.
19. Ibid., lines 1298–1300.
20. Ibid., lines 1728–29.
21. Ibid., lines 2582–89.
22. Ibid., lines 2593–2603.
23. Marjorie Garber, *Vested Interests: Cross-dressing & cultural anxiety* (New York: Routledge, 1992), p. 32.
24. Myra Jehlen, "Gender," *Critical Terms for Literary Study* ed. Frank Lentricchia and Thomas McLaughlin (Chicago: University of Chicago Press, 1990), p. 272.
25. María Rosa Menocal, in her articles and books (see bibliography), is a particularly strong proponent of the view that the Middle Ages offered a unique period of rapport between the races. Her optimistic view of the period is buttressed by the unprecedented cultural interaction that took place between Jews, Christians and Muslims in Southern France and Spain. Despite this interaction, which is indeed remarkable, popular literature continued to require effacement of cultural difference before social integration could occur.
26. Maŕìa Rosa Menocal, "Signs of the Times: Self, Other and History in *Floire et Blancheflor*," *Romanic Review* 80(4) (1989), p. 502.
27. Iain Higgins, "Imagining Christendom from Jerusalem to Paradis: Asia in Mandeville's Travels," *Discovering New Worlds: Essays on Medieval Exploration and Imagination*, ed. Scott D. Westrem (New York: Garland, 1991), p. 93.
28. *La lettre du Prêtre Jean*, ed. Martin Gosman (Groningen: Bouma's Boekhuis, 1982), lines 1149–51.
29. Ibid., lines 1152–58.
30. Mary Campbell, *The Witness and the Other World: Exotic European Travel Writing 400-1600* (Ithaca: Cornell UP, 1989), p. 124.
31. *La fille du comte de Ponthieu*, ed. C. Brunel, (Paris: Champion CFMA, 1926), lines 555–59.
32. Ibid., lines 562–4.
33. Ibid., p. 126.
34. Ibid., p. 126.

8. Conclusions

Through the Middle Ages, the relationship between Saracens and Christians went through many changes in both reality and in literature. Trends in categorizing the Muslim Other emerge, from desire and destruction to integration and, finally, to rejection. However, these trends represent no more than broad movements—certainly not neat categories. While perhaps composed at different times, many of the stories circulated simultaneously, some indicating a high degree of acceptation of the Christian-Muslim union while others offered little hope for such alliances. The Saracen, at almost all times during the Middle Ages, could play multiple roles. What mattered most in the literature of the period were the relationships he or she was able to form with Christian counterparts.

These relationships, some male-male and other female-male, spoke to concerns that the French had about their own emerging society. As the men faced each other on the literary battlefield, larger-than-life characters played out the conflict between the cultures. The great leader, Gormont, could command the basically good Isembart because the Saracen had many admirable qualities; the French King Louis paled somewhat in comparison. By defeating the formidable Baligant, Charlemagne proved once again that what really counted in life was having God on your side. These epics lent a purpose to the crusades against the Saracen. At the same time, the tales assuaged the feelings of inferiority that confronted the French as they encountered a culture with admittedly attractive armament and architecture.

The male-female relationship opened a new door for exploring cultural contact. The battle between the sexes is a subtler one, allowing for examination of difference in more detail than the shouting of insults, or flyting, on the battlefield. Troubadour poetry converted distance into desire. The beloved needed not be (indeed could not be) in close proximity to the lover. Language served as an obstacle between the lovers, and the obstacle itself motivated desire. Tension and interest arose from the inability of the two cultures to meet, and should they meet, to communicate. Love arose from the unknown and unattainable.

By the late twelfth and thirteenth centuries, the West had come to know a great deal more about Islam. Crusades had brought the two cultures into contact and trading and political relationships were formed. As a result, literary depictions allowed contact beyond conflict between Christian and Muslim. The bedroom replaced the battlefield as the site of interaction, as the Saracen princess became the wife of choice for the crusading French literary hero. Canon law reflected new cultural mores, dictating how interreligious and interethnic relationships were to be conducted. Travel to the otherworld, the East, dominated the literary scene.

By the late thirteenth and fourteenth centuries, stories of fascination with the East began exposing the difficulties of cross-cultural relationships. Heroines marrying into French aristocracy, like Nicolette, had to reject their Saracen heritage definitively. National boundaries replaced regional ones, and a sense of national belonging surfaced among the literary characters of the period. While the thirteenth-century *Fille du comte de Ponthieu* appreciates the kindness of her Saracen husband and worries about returning among her formerly unkind relatives, the fifteenth-century *Fille* has undergone a transformation. She has waited to return to her "natural law" for years, and displays a remarkable cruelty toward the Saracen ruler who has been her loving husband for years. Love between cultures has moved from the exotic to the unnatural.

This general trend in the treatment of the Saracen certainly does not encompass all works of the French Middle Ages. *Floire et Blancheflor* and *Aucassin et Nicolette*, for instance, are roughly contemporary, yet Floire's integration is made explicit while Nicolette's is not. For centuries, Saracens played the role of the ultimate Other in French society. Their place in French culture was always changing and always dependent upon the exigencies of the text. Saracens could fill any role needed, creating sexual tension among the troubadours and national pride for the counts of Ponthieu.

As the crusades drew to a close in the fifteenth century, the Saracen had been explored, examined, and finally rejected as a source of inspiration for the medieval author. Attention turned from the external threat, which had largely disappeared, to the internal threat; namely, England. The Saracens were on the run, to be driven conclusively from the continent by 1492. Christendom, however, was embroiled in internal conflict. The Avignon-Rome schism of the fourteenth-century Church left the French more concerned with fighting the Christian Other than the Muslim Other. The Hundred Years' War dominated the late fourteenth and early fifteenth century.

This conflict between Christians meant that the French could no longer use the Saracen as the only means of national self-definition. The hostility between Christian and Muslim was neither the only nor the most important disharmony. Kevin Brownlee has explored the movement as the French shifted focus from the Other without to the Other within.[1] Brownlee locates the shift in perspective in the late fourteenth to early fifteenth centuries. He compares two of Philippe de Mézières' E*pistres* to a *ditié* about Joan of Arc by Christine de Pizan. Philippe focuses on similarity between the warring English and French in order to encourage the launching of a new crusade against the Infidel. Christine, however, relocates the crusade from the Holy Land to France. Joan of Arc is fashioned as a crusader against the evil English. Chosen by God and with his help, she will conquer the English, reform the Church and finally retake the Holy Land. The enemy is no longer the Saracen, but the heretic within the Christian brotherhood, the English.

The generic transformations that took place from the *Chanson de Roland* to the final redaction of the *Fille du comte de Ponthieu* are many and varied. As authors continually tried new ways of exploring new relationships, they necessarily developed genres that had not been seen before in French literature. The richness that Arab culture lent to the West included not only material goods and linguistic or literary borrowing, but also a pervasive, imaginary Other that allowed the French to construct their own identity. The search for the origins of French literature will doubtless find more material evidence of sharing between France and the Muslim world. However, the huge literary debt to Arab culture speaks from within the pages of the medieval French text in the ever-present and ever-formative interethnic couple.

NOTES

1. Kevin Brownlee, "Cultural Comparison: Crusade as Construct in Late Medieval France," *L'Esprit Créateur*. 32 (3) (1992), pp. 13–24.

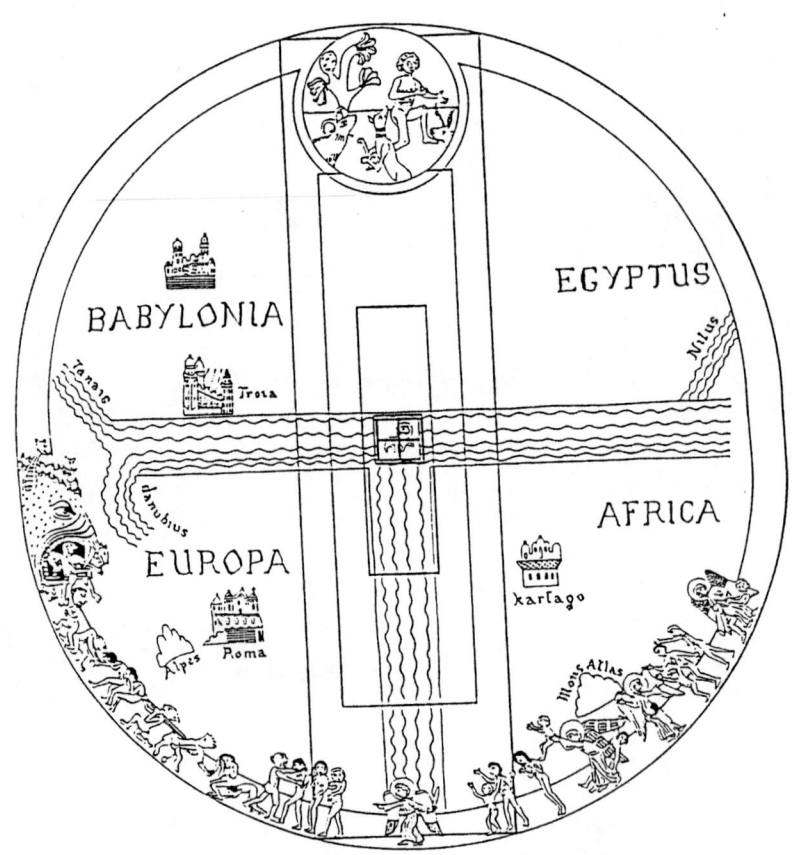

Figure 1 - *Orbis Terrae* (D. Lecoq, J.-P, Magnier)

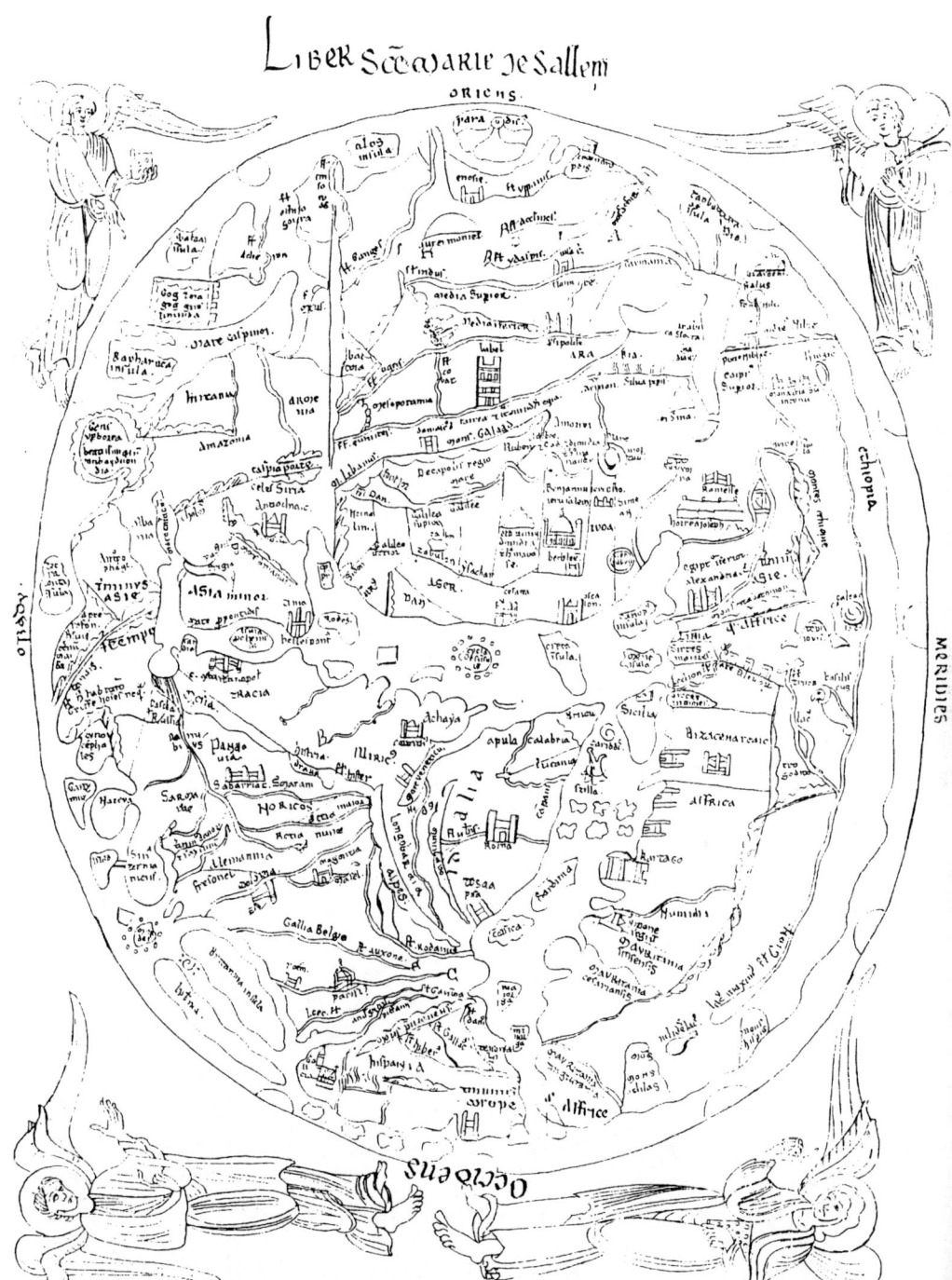

Figure 2 – Cambridge, Corpus Christi College, ms 66, fol. 2

Bibliography

Primary Sources

Alexandre de Paris. *Le roman d'Alexandre*. Paris: Livre de Poche Lettres Gothiques, 1994.

Aliscans, ed. C. Régnier. 2 vols. Paris: Champion, 1990.

Amato di Monte Cassino. *Storia de Normanni*. trans. into Old French by Vincent of Bartholomaeis. In "Storia de' Normanni di Amato di Montecassino volgarizzata in antico francese". *Fonti per la storia d'Italia, pubblicata dall' Istituto storico italiano per il Medio Evo. Scrittori. Secolo XI*. Rome: Tipografia del Senato, 1935.

Amt, Emily, ed. *Women's Lives in Medieval Europe: A Sourcebook*. New York: Routledge, 1993.

Anseïs de Carthage: chanson de geste du XIIe siècle. Paris: Sociéte française d'éditions littéraires et techniques, 1938.

Archives municipales de Bordeaux I. "L'histoire de Cenebrun et Fenix." In *Livre des Bouillons*. Bordeaux: Imprimérie G. Gounouilhou, 1867: 473–83.

Aucassin et Nicolette. Ed. J. Dufournet. Paris: Champion CFMA, 1973.

Aucassin et Nicolette. ed. Mario Roques. Paris: Champion, 1968.

Augustine. *Faith and Works*. trans. Gregory J. Lombardo. NY, NY: Newman Press, 1988.

Bond, Gerald A. *The Poetry of William VII, Count of Poitiers, IX Duke of Aquitaine*. NY: Garland, 1982.

Buridant, Claude, ed. *La Traduction du Pseudo-Turpin du ms. Vatican Regina 624*. Geneva: Droz, 1976.

La Chanson de Roland. ed. Joseph Bédier. Paris: Union Générale d'Éditions, 1982.

La Chanson de Guillaume. ed. F. Suard. Classiques Garnier. Paris: Bordas, 1991.

Les Chansons de Guillaume IX, duc d'Aquitaine. ed. A. Jeanroy. Paris: Champion, 1927. Chibnall, Marjorie, trans. Orderic Vital's Ecclesiastical History. Oxford: Clarendon Press, 1968–80: V. 358–79.

Constable, Giles, ed. The Letters of Peter the Venerable. Cambridge, MA: Harvard University Press, 1967.

Conte de Floire et Blancheflor. Ed. J.-L. Leclanche. Paris: Champion CFMA, 1983.

Le conte de Floire et Blancheflor. Modern French translation with foreword and notes. Ed. J.-L. Leclanche. Paris: Champion CFMA, 1986.

Dozy, Reinhart Pieter Anne. Recherches sur l'histoire et la littérature de l'Espagne pendant le moyen âge. Leyde: E. J. Brill, 1881.

Enfances Guillaume. Ed. P. Henry. Paris: Champion, 1935.

La Fille du comte de Ponthieu. Ed. C. Brunel. Paris: Champion CFMA, 1926.

Fierabras, eds. A. Stimming, A. Hilka, A. de Mandach. Habstetten, 1891.

Fierabras, eds. A. Kroeber and G. Servois. Paris: F. Vieweg, 1860.

Floire et Blancheflor, ed. J.-L. Leclanche. Paris:Champion, 1980.

La Geste de Fierabras. ed. A. de Mandach. Geneva: Droz, 1987.

Gormont et Isembart. ed. Alphonse Bayot. Paris:Champion, 1931.

Gratian. Decretum Magistri Gratiani. In Corpus iuris canonici. Ed. E. Friedberg. 2 vols. Graz: Akademische Druck-u. Verlagsanstalt, 1955.

Hugh of Saint-Victor. De Arca Noe Mystica. Ed. Migne. Patrologia Latina 176: 681–704.

Kline, Galen R. The Voyage d'Outremer by Bertrandon de la Broquière. NY: Peter Lang, 1988.

La lettre du Prêtre Jean. Ed. Martin Gosman. Groningen: Bouma's Boekhuis, 1982.

La Sale, Antoine de. Paradis, Excursion et Géographie. F. Mora-Lebrun, trans. Paris 1983.

Letts, M., ed. Mandeville's Travels, Texts and Translations. London: Hakluyt Society, 1953.

Lieutaud, V., ed. Lou Roman d'Arle in Notes pour servir à l'histoire de la Provence, fasc. 4. Marseille 1873–74.

Lion de Bourges: poème épique du XIVe siècle. Ed. W. W. Kibler, Picheret, Fenster. 2 vols. Geneva: Droz, 1980.

Lombard, Peter. Sententiarum libri IV. 3rd edition. Grottaferrata : Editiones Collegii S. Bonaventurae ad Claras Aquas, 1971–1981.

"Mainet." ed. Gaston Paris. Romania 4 (1875): 303–337.

Melville, Charles and Ahmad Ubaydli, Christians and Moors in Spain: Volume III Arabic Sources (711–1501). Warminster, England: Aris & Phillips, 1992.

Migne, Jacques-Paul. Patrologiae cursus completus omnium. Turnholti, Belgium: Brepols, 1911 (referred to as PL).

Prise de Defur et le voyage d'Alexandre au paradis terrestre. Ed. L.P.G. Peckham and M.S. La Du. Elliott Monographs 35. Princeton and Paris: PUP and PUF, 1935.

La Prise d'Orange: Chanson de geste de la fin du XIIe siècle. ed. Claude Régnier. Paris: Éditions Klincksieck, 1972.

Le Roman de Renart. Paris: J. de Bonnot, 1975.
Las Siete Partidas, trans. Samuel Parsons Scott. Chicago: American Bar Association, 1931.
Le Siège de Barbastre. ed. J.L. Perrier. Paris: Champion, 1926.
Smith, Colin. Christians and Moors in Spain: Volume I (711–1150). Warminster, England: Aris & Phillips, 1988.
The Songs of Jaufré Rudel. ed. Rupert Pickens. Toronto: University of Toronto Press, 1977.
The Usatges of Barcelona. trans. Donald J. Kagay. Philadelphia: University of Pennsylvania Press, 1994.
Walpole, Ronald N., ed. An Anonymous Old French Translation of the Pseudo-Turpin Chronicle. Cambridge, MA: Medieval Academy of America, 1979.
———. "The Burgundian Translation of the Pseudo-Turpin Chronicle in the Bibliothèque Nationale (French ms 25438)." Romance Philology 2 (1) (1948): 177–215.
Winterbottom, M., trans. The Elder Seneca Declamations in Two Volumes. Cambridge: Harvard University Press, 1974.
Wolf and Rosenstein. The Poetry of Cercamon and Jaufré Rudel. New York: Garland, 1983.

Secondary Sources

Amerlinckz, Frans and Megay, Joyce, ed. Travel, Quest, and Pilgrimage as a Literary Theme: Studies in Honor of Reino Virtanen. Manhattan, KS: Society of Spanish and Spanish-American Studies; Ann Arbor, Mich. : distributed by University Microfilms International, 1978.
Antoine, Regis. "La relation exotique." In Revue des sciences humaines, 147, (juillet–sept., 1972), 373–385.
Anderson, Bonnie S. and Judith P. Zinsser. A History of Their Own, Vol. I. New York: Harper and Row, 1988.
Ashcroft, Bill. "Constitutive Graphonomy." In The Post-Colonial Studies Reader. Eds. Bill Ashcroft, Gareth Griffiths, Helen Tiffin. New York: Routledge, 1995: 298–302.
Bancourt, Paul. Les musulmans dans les chansons de geste du Cycle du roi. Aix-en-Provence: Université de Provence; Marseille: J. Laffitte, 1982.
Bédier, Joseph. "La Composition de la Chanson de Fierabras." Romania 17 (1888): 22–51.
Bédier, Joseph. Les legendes épiques. 3rd ed. Paris: Champion, 1926–29.
Beech, George T. "Troubadour Contacts with Muslim Spain and Knowledge of Arabic: New Evidence Concerning William IX of Aquitaine." Romania 113 (1992–95): 14–42.
Bennett, Philip. "The Storming of the Other World, the Enamoured Muslim Princess, and the Evolution of the Legend of Guillaume d'Orange," Guillaume d'Orange and the Chanson de Geste. Ed. Wolfgang Emden. Reading: Société Rencesvals, 1984: 1–14.

Bezzola, Renato R. *Les Origines et la formation de la littérature courtoise en Occident* (500–1200). 3 vols. Paris: Champion, 1966.

Bhabha, Homi K. "Of Mimicry and Man: The Ambivalence of Colonial Discourse" in *October* 28 (1984)125–33.

———, ed. *Nation and Narration*. London: Routledge, 1990.

———. "The Other Question: The Stereotype and Colonial Discourse." In *The Politics of Theory*. ed. Francis Barker. Colchester: University of Essex, 1983.

Bloch, R. Howard. "842. The First Document and the Birth of Medieval Studies." In *A New History of French Literature*. ed. D. Hollier. Cambridge: Harvard University Press, 1989: 6–13.

———. *Medieval Misogyny*. Chicago: University of Chicago Press, 1991.

Brownlee, Kevin. "Cultural Comparison: Crusade as Construct in Late Medieval France." *L'Esprit Créateur*. 32 (3) (1992):13–24.

Bullough, Vern L. "On Being Male in the Middle Ages." In *Medieval Masculinities: Regarding Men in the Middle Ages*. Ed. Clare Lees. Minneapolis: University of Minnesota Press, 1994.

Burns, E. Jane. *Bodytalk*. Philadelphia: University of Pennsylvania Press, 1993.

Butterfield, Ardis. "Medieval genres and modern genre theory." *Paragraph*. 13 (1990): 184–201.

Butor, Michel, "Le voyage et l'écriture" in *Romantisme* 4 (1972): 14–19.

Campbell, Kimberlee Anne. "Fighting Back: a survey of patterns of female agressiveness in the Old French chansons de geste." In *Charlemagne in the North*. ed. Philip Bennett, Anne E. Cobby and Graham Runnalls. Edinburgh: Société Rencesvals, 1993: 241–52.

Campbell, Mary. *The Witness and the Other World: Exotic European Travel Writing 400–1600*. Ithaca: Cornell UP, 1989.

Chittick, William. *The Sufi Path of Knowledge*. Albany: SUNY Press, 1989.

Clark, Robert L. A. and Claire Sponsler. "Queer Play: The Cultural Work of Crossdressing in Medieval Drama." *New Literary History*. 28 (2) (1997): 319–44.

———. "Othered Bodies: Racial Cross-Dressing in the Mistere de la Sainte Hostie and the Croxton Play of the Sacrament." *Journal of Medieval and Early Modern Studies*. 29 (1) (1999): 61–87.

Comfort, William Wistar. "The Literary Rôle of the Saracens in the French Epic." PMLA 55 (1940 supplement): 628–59.

Connochie-Bourgne, Chantal. "L'Orient, réalité et discours, dans l'*Image du Monde*." *Images et signes de l'Orient dans l'Occident médiéval*. Ed. Arrouye. *Sénéfiance* 11. Aix-en-Provence: Université de Provence, 1982.

Crespi, Gabriele. *The Arabs in Europe*. New York: Rizzoli, 1986.

d'Alverny, Marie-Thérèse, *La connaissance de l'Islam dans l'Occident médi´éval*. Brookfield, Vt: Variorum, 1994.

Daniel, Norman. *Heroes and Saracens: an interpretation of the chansons de geste*. Edinburgh: Edinburgh University Press, 1984.

Bibliography

———. *Islam and the West: the making of an image*. Edinburgh: University Press, 1984.

Deluz, Christiane. "Le paradis terrestre, image de l'orient lointain dans quelques documents géographiques médiévaux." *Images et signes de l'Orient dans l'Occident médiéval*. Ed. Arrouye. Sénéfiance 11. Aix-en-Provence: Université de Provence, 1982: 145–161.

de Weever, Jacqueline. "Nicolette's Blackness: Lost in Translation." *Romance Notes* 34 (1994): 317–25.

———. *Sheba's Daughters: Whitening and Demonizing the Saracen Woman in Medieval French Epic*. New York: Garland, 1998.

Dijkstra, Cathrynke and Martin Gosman. "Poetic Fiction and Poetic Reality: the Case of the Romance Crusade Lyrics." *Neophilologus* 79 (1995): 13–24.

Duby, Georges. *The Knight, the Lady and the Priest: The Making of Modern Marriage in Medieval France*. Trans. Barbara Bray. New York: Pantheon, 1983.

Dufournet, Jean. *Aucassin et Nicolette*. Critical edition. Paris: Garnier-Flammarion, 1973.

Duggan, J.J. *A Guide to Studies on the Chanson de Roland*. London: Grant & Cutler, 1976.

Edmonds, Barbara P. "Le portrait des Sarrasins dans la Chanson de Roland." *French Review*. 44 (5) (1971): 870–81.

Esmein, Adhemar. *Le mariage en droit canonique*. Essays in history, economics and social science. New York: Burt Franklin, 1968.

Fanon, Frantz. *Les damnés de la terre*. Paris: Gallimard, 1991.

———. *Peau noire, masques blancs*. Paris: Éditions du Seuil, 1952.

Faral, Edmond. "Introduction." *Dictionnaire des lettres françaises: le Moyen Age*. Ed. Bossuat et. al. Paris: Fayard, 1992.

Favier, Jean. *Les Grandes découvertes d'Alexandre à Magellen*. Paris: Fayard, 1991.

Fletcher, Richard. *Moorish Spain*. London: Weidenfeld & Nicolson, 1992.

Frank, Grace. "The Distant Love of Jaufré Rudel." *Modern Language Notes* 57 (1942).

Frank, Istvàn. "*Babariol babarian* dans Guillaume IX." *Romania* 73 (1952): 227–234.

Frantzen, Allen. "When Women Aren't Enough." *Speculum*. 68 (2) (1993): 445–71.

Garber, Marjorie. *Vested Interests: Cross-dressing & cultural anxiety*. New York: Routledge, 1992.

Garreau, Joseph E. "Et si Aucassin et Nicolette n'était qu' 'une histoire d'amour fort simple'?" *Modern Language Studies*. 15(4)1985: 184–193.

Gates, Henry Louis. "Race," *Writing and Difference*. Chicago: UCP, 1986.

Gaudemet, Jean. *Le Mariage en Occident*. Paris: Cerf, 1987.

Gaunt, Simon. "From Epic to Romance: Gender and Sexuality in the *Roman d'Enéas*." *Romanic Review*. 83 (1) (1992): 1–27.

Grenier, Jean. "Le voyage (Etude phénoménologique)" NRF 138, (juin, 1964), 1000–10.

Grosrichard, Alain. *Structure du sérail: la fiction du despotisme asiatique dans l'Occident classique*. Paris: Éditions du Seuil, 1979.

Hatem, Anouar. *Les poèmes épiques des croisades: genèse, historicité, localisation*. Paris: P. Geuthner, 1932.

Higgins, Iain. "Imagining Christendom from Jerusalem to Paradis: Asia in Mandeville's Travels." In *Discovering New Worlds: Essays on Medieval Exploration and Imagination*. Ed. Scott D. Westrem. New York: Garland, 1991: 91–114.

hooks, bell. *Yearning: Race, Gender and Cultural Politics*. Boston: South End Press, 1990.

Hotchkiss, Valerie. "Gender Transgression and the Abandoned Wife." In *Gender Rhetorics: Postures of Dominance and Submission in History*. Ed. Richard C. Trexler. Binghamton, NY: Center for Medieval Texts and Studies, 1994: 207–18.

Hunt, Tony. "La Parodie médiévale : le cas d'Aucassin et Nicolette." *Romania* 100 (1979): 341–381.

———. "Precursors and Progenitors of Aucassin et Nicolette." *Studies in Philology* 74 (1977): 1–19.

Jackson, W. T. H. "The Epic Center as Structural Determinant in Medieval Narrative Poetry." In *The Challenge of the Medieval Text*. ed. Joan M. Ferrante and Robert W. Hanning. NY: Columbia Unversity Press, 1985: 105–84.

JanMohamed, Abdul R. "The Economy of Manichean Allegory: The Function of Racial Difference in Colonialist Literature." *Critical Inquiry* 12(1) (1985): 59–87.

Jauss, Hans Robert. *Toward an Aesthetic of Reception*. trans. Timothy Bahti. Minneapolis: University of Minnesota Press, 1982.

Jehlen, Myra. "Gender." In *Critical Terms for Literary Study*. Ed. Frank Lentricchia and Thomas McLaughlin. Chicago: University of Chicago Press, 1990: 263–273.

Jones, C. Meredith. "The Conventional Saracen of the Songs of Geste." *Speculum* 17 (1942): 201–225.

Kay, Sarah. "Continuation as Criticism: The Case of Jaufre Rudel." *Medium Aevum*. 56(1) (1987): 46–64.

———. "La représentation de la féminité dans les chansons de geste." In *Charlemagne in the North*. ed. Philip Bennett, Anne E. Cobby and Graham Runnalls. Edinburgh: Société Rencesvals, 1993: 223–40.

———. *The Chansons de Geste in the Age of Romance*. Oxford: Clarendon Press, 1995.

Keller, Hans-Erich. "La belle Sarrasine dans Fierabras et ses dérivés." In *Charlemagne in the North*. ed. Philip Bennett, Anne E. Cobby and Graham Runnalls. Edinburgh: Société Rencesvals, 1993: 299–307.

Ker, Margaret. "Women in Medieval Society." *Exploring Women's Past*. Patrica Crawford, ed. Sydney: George Allen & Unwin, 1983.

Kibler, W. W. "Archetypal Imagery in Floire et Blancheflor." *Romance Quarterly*. 35 (1988): 11–20.

———— "Les personnages féminins dans la geste de Nanteuil." In *Charlemagne in the North*. ed. Philip Bennett, Anne E. Cobby and Graham Runnalls. Edinburgh: Société Rencesvals, 1993: 309–17.

Kinoshita, Sharon. "The Politics of Courtly Love: La Prise d'Orange and the Conversion of the Saracen Queen," *Romanic Review* 86 (2) (1995): 265-287.

Knudson, Charles A. "Le thème de la princesse sarrasine dans La Prise d'Orange." *Romance Philology* 22(4) (1969): 449–62.

Koht, Halvdan. "The Dawn of Nationalism in Europe" *American Historical Review* 52 (1946–47): 265–80.

Lauer, Philippe. "Louis IV d'Outre-mer et le fragment d'Isembart et Gormont." *Romania*. 26 (1897): 161–74.

Le Goff, Jacques. *L'imaginaire médiéval*. Paris: Gallimard, 1985.

Leclanche, J.-L. *Contribution à l'Étude de la transmission des plus anciennes oeuvres romanesques françaises. Un cas privilégié: Floire et Blancheflor*. Thesis Paris-Sorbonne. Lille, 1980.

Lecoq, Danielle. "La 'mappemonde' du *De Arca Noe Mystica* de Hugues de Saint-Victor (1128–29)" *Géographie du monde au Moyen âge et à la Renaissance*. Ed. Monique Pelletier. Paris: Editions du comité des Travaux Historiques et Scientifiques, 1989.

Lefèvre, Yves. "L'Amors de Terra Lonhdana dans les chansons de Jaufré Rudel." In *Mélanges offerts à Rita Lejeune*. Gembloux: Duculot, 1968: 185–196.

Lévi-Provençal, E. "Poésie arabe d'Espagne et poésie d'Europe médiévale." In *Islam d'Occident Études d'histoire médiévale*. Paris: G.P. Maisonneuve, 1948.

Liborio, Mariantonia, trans. *Aucassin et Nicolette*. Torino: Einaudi, 1976.

Lot, Ferdinand. "Gormond et Isembart: recherches sur les fondements historiques de cette épopée." *Romania*. 27 (1898): 1–54.

Lowe, Lisa. *Critical Terrains: French and British Orientalisms*. Ithaca: Cornell UP, 1991.

Lynn, Thérèse B. "Pour une réhabilitation d'Eve". *The French Review*. 48 (1975): 870–876.

Mandach, A. de. *La Geste de Charlemagne et de Roland*. Geneva: Droz, 1961.

Massignon, Louis. "L'Occident devant l'Orient: Primauté d'une solution culturelle" in *Opera Minora* I.

Menocal, María Rosa. "Signs of the Times: Self, Other and History in *Aucassin et Nicolette*. *Romanic Review*. 80(4) (1989): 497–511.

————. *The Arabic Role in Medieval Literary History: A Forgotten Heritage*. Philadelphia: University of Pennsylvania Press, 1979.

————. *Shards of Love*. Durham, NC: Duke University Press, 1994.

Meredith-Jones, C. "The Conventional Saracen of the Songs of Geste." *Speculum* 17 (1942): 201–25.

Micha, A. "En relisant 'Aucassin et Nicolette'" *De la Chanson de geste au roman*. Geneva: Droz, 1976. 465–478.

Mollat, M. *Les Explorateurs du XIIe au XIIIe siècle*. Paris: J.C. Lattes, 1984.

Muldoon, James. *Popes, Lawyers, and Infidels: the Church and the non-Christian world, 1250–1550*. Philadelphia: University of Pennsylvania Press, 1979.

Ollier, Marie-Louise. "Demande Sociale et Constitution d'un 'Genre': la situation dans la France du XIIe siècle." *Mosaic*. 8 (4) (1975): 205–216.

Paris, Gaston. *Romania* 31 (1902): 445–6.

Paterson, Linda M. "Stéréotypes géographiques et éthniques en Occitanie au XIIe et XIIIe siècles." *Actes 2e congrès internationale de l'association internationale d'études occitanes.* 1987.

Perret, Michèle. "Travesties et Transsexuelles: Yde, Silence, Grisandole, Blanchandine." *Romance Notes* 25(3) (1984–85): 328–40.

Rajna, Pio. "La badia di Niort." *Romania*, 6 (1876), 249–53.

Ramey, Lynn Tarte. "Role Models? Saracen Women in Medieval French Epic." *Romance Notes*. forthcoming.

Rey, G. de. *Les Invasions des Sarrasins en Provence*. Marseille: Lafitte, 1971.

Roques, Mario. "Le Roman d'Arles." *Histoire Littéraire Française*. 38 (1949): 606–41.

———. *La Geste de Fierabras*. Geneva: Droz, 1987.

Rosenstein, Roy. "New Perspectives on Distant Love: Jaufré Rudel, Uc Bru, and Sarrazina." *Modern Philology* 87 (3) (1990): 225–238.

Said, Edward. *Culture and Imperialism*. New York: Knopf, 1993.

Samaran, C. "Lectures sous les rayons ultraviolets." *Romania* 53 (1927): 291–7.

Schulze-Busacker, Elisabeth. "French Conceptions of Foreigners and Foreign Languages in the 12th and 13th Centuries." *Romance Philology* 41 (1987): 24–47.

Sénac, Philippe. *L'image de l'autre: histoire de l'occident médiéval face à Islam*. Paris: Flammarion, 1983

Spiegel, Gabrielle M. *Romancing the Past: the rise of vernacular prose historiography in 13th-century France*. Berkeley: UCP, 1993.

Spitzer, Leo. "L'Amour lointain de Jaufré Rudel." *Romanische Literaturstudien*. Tübingen: M. Niemeyer, 1959.

Stanesco, Michel. "L'étrange aventure d'un faux muet : blessures symboliques et performances sexuelles dans un poème de Guillaume IX d'Aquitaine." *Cahiers de Civilisation Médiévale*. 32 (2) (1989):115–124.

Tattersall, Jill. "Shifting Perspectives and the Illusion of Reality in *Aucassin et Nicolette*. *French Studies*. 38 (3) (1984): 257–267.

Thiong'o, Ngugi wa, *Homecoming: Essays*. London: Heinemann, 1972.

Uhl, Patrice. "*Farai un vers, pos mi sonelh* : la version du chansonnier C (B.N., Fr. 856), la cobla bilingue et le problème du *lati* ou *Tarrababart saramahart* dans Guillaume IX d'Aquitaine." *Cahiers de Civilisation Médiévale*. 33 (1) (1990): 19–42.

Vallecalle, Jean-Claude. "Rupture et intégration: l'héroïne révoltée dans les chansons de geste." In *Charlemagne in the North*. ed. Philip Bennett, Anne E. Cobby and Graham Runnalls. Edinburgh: Société Rencesvals, 1993: 449–61.

Vance, Eugene. "*Aucassin et Nicolette* as a Medieval Comedy of Signification and Exchange." *The Nature of Medieval Narrative*. Ed. Grunmann-Gaudet. Lexington, KY: French Forum, 1980: 57–76.

———. "The Word at Heart: *Aucassin et Nicolette* as a Medieval Comedy of Language." *Yale French Studies*. 45 (1970): 33–51.

———. *Mervelous Signals*. Lincoln: University of Nebraska Press, 1986.

Warren, F. M. "The Enamoured Saracen Princess in Orderic Vital and the French Epic." PMLA 28 (1914): 341–58.

Weeks, Raymond. "The Siège de Barbastre". *Romanic Review* 10 (4) (1919):287–321, continued in 11 (4) (1920): 349–369 and 12 (4) (1921): 155–167.

Westrem, Scott D., ed. *Discovering New Worlds: Essays on Medieval Exploration and Imagination*. NY: Garland, 1991.

Ziolkowski, Jan M. *Talking Animals: medieval Latin beast poetry, 750–1150*. Philadelphia: University of Pennsylvania Press, 1993.

Index

Ab lo temps qe.s fai refreschar (Cercamon), 23-24
Agolant, 61, 63
al-Bakri, 20
Alexander III, Pope, 58
Alfonso VI, 63-64
Alfonso X, 36
Alis, 68, 87-89, 91
Aliscans, 38, 39, 42-43, 46-47
Amatus of Montecassino, 20, 58
amor de lonh, 26, 28
Anderson, Bonnie S., 45
Anonymous of Béthune, 15
Arabic:
    language, 19
    sources in French literature, 1, 19
Ashcroft, Bill, 31
Aucassin et Nicolette, 5, 6, 68, 71, 76-80, 83, 85-86, 98
Aucassin, 71. See also Aucassin et Nicolette

Babel, tower of, 72, 75
baptism, 57, 65
Barbastro. See siege of Barbastro
battle, 7, 103 See also siege
    of Roncevaux, 7
    of Saucourt, 14

Beatus de Morgan, 35, 42
Bédier, Joseph, 1, 39
Bennett, Philip, 70
Beuves de Commarcis, 54
Bhabha, Homi, 3
Blancheflor, 68, 71. See also Floire et Blancheflor
Bloch, R. Howard, 45
Bohemond, 39
Bramimonde, 43, 63
Brownlee, Kevin, 103
Bullough, Vern L., 84
Burns, E. Jane, 47

canon law, 53
captivity, 59
cartography, 72-73
category:
    crisis of, 91
    performative 92
Cercamon, 23-24, 31
Chanson de Guillaume, 37, 68
Chanson de Roland, 1, 7, 9-11, 37, 43, 49, 61, 68, 98, 103
chansons de geste, 5, 35, 38, 45, 59
chantefable, 98. See also Aucassin et Nicolette
Charlemagne, 8, 16, 60, 62, 101
    youth of, 60

Chibnall, Marjorie, 41
Chrétien de Troyes, 45, 77
Clark, Robert L., 86
Compostella, 80
conversion, 49, 56-57, 63, 67
cross-dressing, 83-92
    and class 84-85
    and race 85-87
crusades, 44, 59, 102
cultural assimilation, 50

d'Alverny, Marie-Thérèse, 38
Daniel, Norman, 3
De Arca Noe Mystica (Hugh of Saint-Victor), 73
de Weever, Jacqueline, 86
Decretum (Gratian), 53
disguise, 78
Dijkstra, Cathrynke, 32
disputationes, 53
Duby, Georges, 53

Eleanor of Aquitaine, 22, 44-45
epic, 7-16, 32, 49, 50 See also romance epic
    center, 16
    genre of battle, 4, 5

Fanon, Frantz, 3, 47, 63
Farai un vers, pos me sonelh (William IX), 20-23
Faral, E., 72
Favier, Jean, 79
female rule, 44
Fierabras, 46
Fille du comte de Ponthieu, 5, 68, 93-98,103
Floire et Blancheflor, 5, 68, 71, 74, 76-80, 83, 89-92, 98-99, 102
Foucon de Candie, 42
Frank, Grace, 26
Frank, István, 21
Frantzen, Allen, 83
Fulcher of Chartre, 95

Galienne, 62
Garber, Marjorie, 91
Gaudemet, Jean, 53
Gazan, Mongal chief, 67
Genghis Khan, 67
genre. *See also* epic, chantefable, troubadour poetry, romance
    epic hybrid, 5, 99
geography, 69-77, 98
Girart, 56-57
Gloriete, 48, 70
Gloris, 90-91
Gog and Magog, 72, 75
Gormont et Isembart, 5, 13-16, 37, 68, 98, 101-02
Gosman, Martin, 32
Gratian of Bologna, 53-59
Guibourc, 4, 37-39, 41-43, 48-49, 62, 70, 92
Guillaume d'Orange, 93
Guillaume, of chanson de geste, 48-49, 70

Henri de Mayence, 75
Henry I, 44
Henry II, 45
Higgins, Iain, 94
Historia Ecclesiastica (Orderic Vitalis), 39
Historia Hierosolymitana, 95
Historia Karoli Magni et Rotholandi, 60
Hotchkiss, Valerie, 84
Hugh of Saint-Victor, 73
Hungary, conversion of, 79
hybrid text, 15

Ibn al-'Arabî, 27
Ibn Hayyan, 20
imaginary text, 11-16
inheritance, 58-59
integration, 98
Islam: knowledge of, 8-9

JanMohamed, Abdul R., 11, 12
Jaufré Rudel, 24, 31

Index

Jauss, Hans Robert, 6
Jean d'Avesnes, 96
Jehlen, Myra, 91
Joan of Arc, 103
Jones, C. Meredith, 38, 42

Kay, Sarah, 25
Ker, Margaret, 44
Khan, Genghis. *See* Genghis Khan
Kibler, William, 79
kidnapping, 54
Kinoshita, Sharon, 50
Knudson, Charles, 42
Koht, Halvdan, 64
Koran, 38

Lacan, Jacques, 4, 11, 93
language:
    in cross-cultural communication, 30
    learning, 61, 92, 96
    problem of, 29, 31, 101
Lanquan li jorn son lonc en mai, 26
Las Siete Partidas, 36, 58-59
Leclanche, J.-L., 74
Lefèvre, Yves, 29
Lévi-Provençal, E., 21
Lion de Bourges, 68, 83, 87-89
Llull, Ramon. *See* Ramon Llull
Lombard, Peter. *See* Peter Lombard
Louis III, 14
Louis VII, 44
Louis VIII, 29
Louis, of chanson de geste, 46, 54, 57, 101
love from afar. *See* amor de lohn

magic, 62
Mainet, 60-61
Malatrie, 46, 55-56, 69
Mandach, A. de, 63
manichean allegory, 11
maps, 72-73, 94
marriage, 45, 63
    and conversion, 56-57
    and integration, 80
    and parental consent, 58
    and succession, 57
    interfaith, 53-60, 83
    roman law, 53
    Paul on, 56-57
Martel, Charles, 7
Maud, 44
Melaz, 39
Menocal, María Rosa, 77, 93
metonymic gap, 32
miscegenation, 23
Mongols, 67
Moniage Guillaume II, 42
Muldoon, James, 59
mysticism, 28, 45

nationalism, 1, 64
Nicolette, 68, 71. *See also Aucassin et Nicolette*
No sap chantar qui so non di, 29

Orable. See Guibourc
Orderic Vitalis, 39
Orientalism, 6

paradise, 72, 76, 95
    anti-, 76
Paris, Gaston, 1
Paul the Apostle, 56
Perret, Michèle, 84, 88
Peter Lombard, 53-58
Peter the Venerable, 38, 63-64
Philippe de Mézières, 103
pilgrimage, 60, 79
Pope Leo, 22
post-colonial:
    critics, 30
    literature, 2
Prester John, 6, 93 letter of, 94
princess, Saracen, 39, 43-50, 71
Prise d'Orange, 5, 37, 50, 70
Pseudo-Turpin Chronicle, 60

Qan lo rius de la fontana (Jaufré Rudel), 24-26

Rainouart, 37, 38, 49
Ramon Llull, 67
rape, 56
raptus, 54-55. *See also* kidnapping; captivity
Reconquest, 12, 38
regionalism, 1
religion, 49
Roman d'Alexandre, 76
Roman law, 56-57
romance epic, 5, 35-50, 50
Rudel, Jaufré. *See* Jaufré Rudel

Saint James of Compostella, 60
Saladin, 96, 98
Saracen:
    as mirrors of the French, 37
    black, 46-47, 86
    definition of, 8
    feminization of, 64
    white, 11, 45, 48-49
    See also princess, Saracen
Schulze-Busacker, Elisabeth, 61
Sénac, Philippe, 3, 37, 38, 42-43, 74
Seneca, 39
Senteniae (Peter Lombard), 53
seraglio, 70
sexuality, 48
Siege de Barbastre, 45, 48, 53, 69
siege of Barbastro, 19, 54, 56, 58
Siete Partidas, Las. *See Las Siete Partidas*
Simon de Monfort, 29
Spiegel, Gabrielle, 3, 6, 36
Spitzer, Leo, 26
Sponsler, Claire, 86
symbolic text, 11-16

Thibaut, 42, 48
Thiong'o, Ngugi Wa, 30
T-O map, 72
tolerance, 92

topsy-turvy world, 77
Torelore, 76
translation, 38, 60
transvestism. *See* cross-dressing
travel, 2, 68, 71-80, 83, 93-95, 98
    and self-identity, 92
    as self-discovery, 83
    time, 79
traveler, 78, 79
troubadour poetry, 49, 101-02
Turmon, 14

Uhl, Patrice, 21
Usatges de Barcelona, 54

Vance, Eugene, 78
vida, 26
Voyage d'Alexandre au Paradis terrestre, 76

warfare. *See* battle
Warren, F. M., 39
Weeks, Raymond, 70
William IX, Duke of Aquitaine, 20-23, 45, 54
William of Ver, 94
William V (grandfather of William IX), 22
William VII, Count of Poitiers. *See* William, IX Duke of Aquitaine
woman:
    Christian versus Saracen 43-44
    on a pedestal motif, 23, 45

Zaïda, 63
Zinnser, Judith P., 45
Ziolkowski, Jan, 22